Advance Praise for
Vegan Meal Plan fo

"Eddie Garza's The 30-Day Vegan Meal Plan for Beginners *is a fabulous resource for anyone seeking to fight climate change with diet change."*

—**Kate Mara**, actress and activist

"We're so lucky to have experienced many of Eddie's delectable, amazing creations personally. The 30-Day Vegan Meal Plan for Beginners *is a must-have for anyone interested in enjoying the many benefits of a plant-based lifestyle. Eddie's recipes are insanely delicious and easy to follow. There's really never been a tastier way to eat healthy and help save the planet."*

—**Daisy Fuentes**, TV host and supermodel, and
Richard Marx, singer-songwriter

"So many people ask me how to start eating vegan, and now I have an easy cookbook I can refer them to!"

—**Daniella Monet**, actress and entrepreneur

"Eddie's journey to improving his health and opening his heart to all living beings will inspire you."

—**Marco Antonio Regil**, TV host and activist

"Chef Eddie Garza's amazing new book, The 30-Day Vegan Meal Plan for Beginners, *is the most comprehensive vegan menu plan on the bookshelves. Eddie will be your expert guide as you eat your way through his yummy recipes. Every ingredient is easily accessible as well as healthy and nutritious. Can everybody say, 'YES!' to Spiced Sweet Potato Cheesecake?"*

—**Chloe Coscarelli**, celebrity chef and author of *Chloe Flavor*

"There are not many chefs who create with so much love as Eddie. I can say that I have tried everything he does, and wow, you would never believe it's vegan! Magnificent. Delicious! Congrats, darling Eddie!"

—**Maria Conchita Alonso**, actress and singer-songwriter

"Eddie has combined health consciousness and our love for flavors and ingredients to adapt our personal kitchens into a lifestyle that protects the planet. The 30-Day Vegan Meal Plan for Beginners *keeps our tummies happy and our hearts clear."*

—**Tai Brown**, actress

"I highly recommend The 30-Day Vegan Meal Plan for Beginners, *especially if you're newly vegan and have a desire to eat healthier and tastier foods than what you've been eating lately."*

—**Vanessa Verduga**, artist and activist

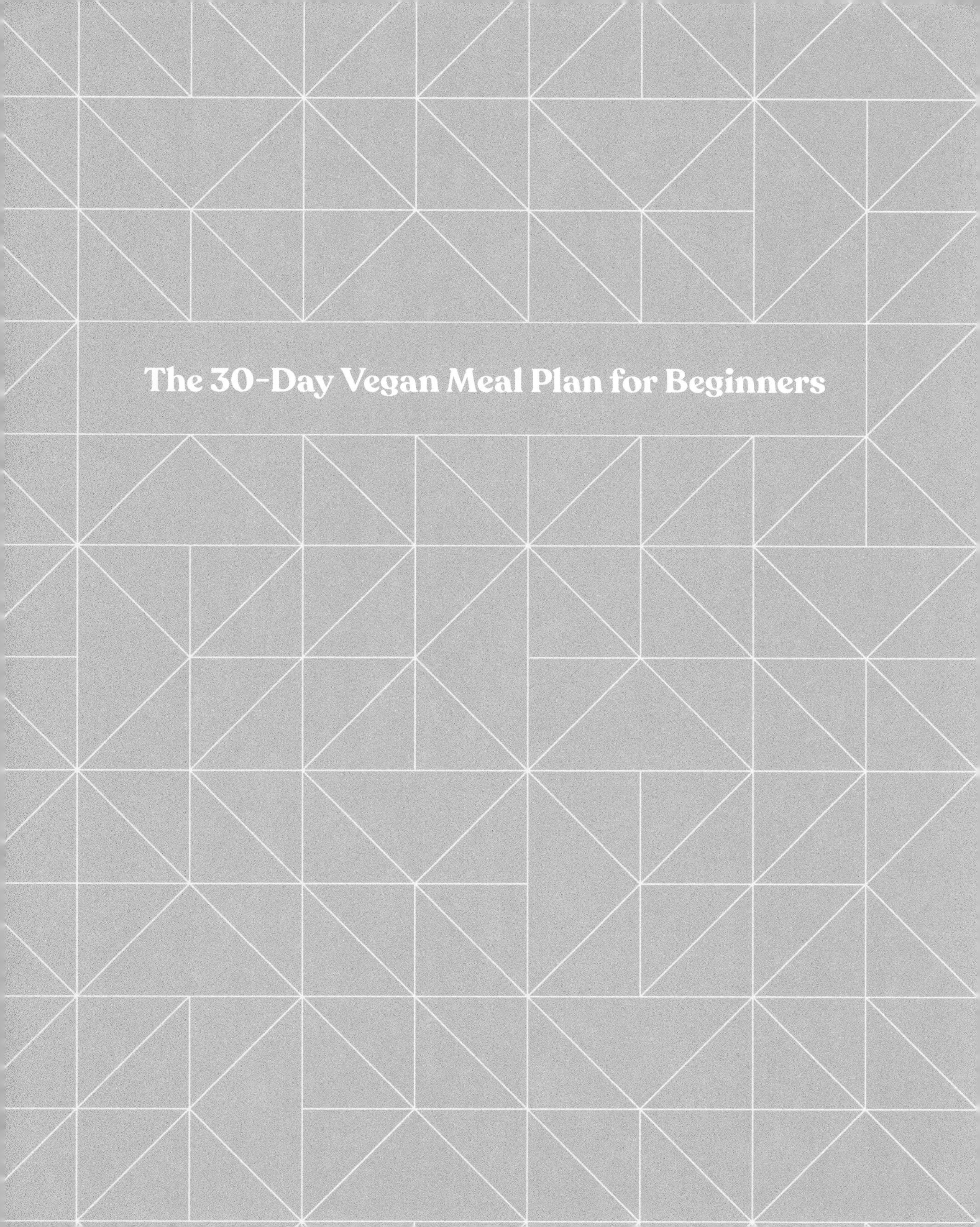

The 30-Day Vegan Meal Plan for Beginners

The 30-Day Vegan Meal Plan for Beginners

Eddie Garza
with Lauren Pitts, MA, RD

Photography by Marija Vidal

For general information on our other products and services or to obtain technical support, please contact our Customer Care Department within the United States at (866) 744-2665, or outside the United States at (510) 253-0500.

Rockridge Press publishes its books in a variety of electronic and print formats. Some content that appears in print may not be available in electronic books, and vice versa.

Interior and Cover Designer: Stephanie Sumulong
Art Producer: Hannah Dickerson
Editor: Cecily McAndrews
Production Editor: Sigi Nacson

Photography © 2020 Marija Vidal; food styling by Victoria Woollard. Decorative pattern © Curly Pat/Creative Market. Author photos courtesy of Enrique Tubio.

ISBN: Print 978-1-64739-754-8 | eBook 978-1-64739-455-4

R0

This is for you, Mom and Dad.

Contents

Introduction x

Part I: The Vegan Primer

Chapter One: What Is the Vegan Diet? 3

Chapter Two: The Health Benefits of a Vegan Diet 11

Chapter Three: Your Vegan Kitchen and Meal Plan 19

Part II: The Recipes

Chapter Four: Breakfast 53

Chapter Five: Salads 67

Chapter Six: Soups and Stews 79

Chapter Seven: Burgers and Sandwiches 91

Chapter Eight: Apps, Sides, and Snacks 105

Chapter Nine: Sauces and Dressings 125

Chapter Ten: Entrées 143

Chapter Eleven: Desserts 167

Measurement Conversions 181

Resources 182

References 184

General Index 187

Recipe Index by Nutrition Label 197

Introduction

Welcome to *The 30-Day Vegan Meal Plan for Beginners*, a step-by-step guide to giving your diet an eco- and animal-friendly makeover. Whether you're here to improve your health, save the planet, or help animals, you're in the right place!

I was born and raised in Texas, a state that takes pride in its meat. When I was growing up, meat-eating was not just a way of life; it was also a competitive sport. By the time I got to college, the idea that meat had to be part of any proper meal was so ingrained in my head that I took it to dangerous heights. Without my mother around to shield me from making poor dietary choices, often lunch was a full pound of bacon from the cafeteria buffet and dinner was usually a large Papa John's meat lover's pizza. And it only got worse.

By the time I started my first career as a music teacher in the Dallas suburbs, I was overindulging in meat and animal products from dawn 'til dusk. Every morning for breakfast, I stopped by Whataburger for a triple cheeseburger and gravy-drenched fries. For lunch, KFC was my poison. Papa John's meat lover's pizza remained a dinner staple. I became dangerously obese, prediabetic, and sick all the time. But it was a habit I couldn't kick. I felt trapped.

One day, a new colleague from Pittsburgh gave me the jolt I needed. Upon introduction, this stranger told me that if I didn't lose weight, I was going to die. I was so embarrassed. I still remember, like it was yesterday, that burning feeling of my face and ears turning beet red. In Texas, people just don't tell you that kind of truth to your face. But she didn't say it out of malice. She simply saw a guy in trouble and wanted to help. So, I accepted her invitation to join her diet support group that weekend.

Over the next few weekends, I learned a lot about the foods we should be putting into our bodies for better health—and everything pointed to plants and away from meat. Study after study showed that people who followed a plant-based diet had lower risk for heart disease, type 2 diabetes, obesity, and other chronic diseases. Together, my new Pittsburgh pal and I started our plant-based journey.

After five years of trial and error, I naturally lost 150 pounds—and kept it off. Now, almost twenty years later, I'm thriving in my second act of life as a plant-based chef and culinary coach. My work has taken me throughout the United States and Latin America to train cooks at hospitals, universities, public schools, and national food chains how to prepare delicious, heart-healthy plant-based foods.

Through my travels, I've met scores of people who say they want to go vegan but don't know where to start. Some folks tell me they tried vegan but quit because they got tired of eating just salads and spaghetti. Others say they wish they could go vegan but could never give up cheese. (*Psst: You don't have to give up cheese anymore!*)

It's for those reasons that I'm excited to present this easy-to-use 30-day meal plan featuring 100 mouthwatering, dietitian-approved vegan recipes. I also show how to cook unique twists on family favorites such as Butternut Squash Mac and Cheese (page 152), Lentil Sloppy Joes (page 94), and Jackfruit Barbecue Sandwiches (page 99). And you won't be skipping dessert, either. From Texas-Style Pineapple-Mango Cobbler (page 170) to Blueberry Cake Donuts with Meyer Lemon Glaze (page 178), I've got your sweet tooth covered. Get ready for a yummy time in your new vegan kitchen!

Part I

The Vegan Primer

Seared Portobello Fajitas, page 153

CHAPTER ONE

What Is the Vegan Diet?

Congratulations on taking your first dive into vegan cooking! Whether you're here for help going fully vegan or simply looking to add more meat-free meals to your culinary repertoire, I promise this journey is going to be a real treat.

I started my vegan journey nearly two decades ago, when soymilk still came in powdered form and vegan cheeses folded instead of melted. Yikes, right? Thankfully, we've come a long way since then! Nowadays, vegan milks dominate the dairy case because they're deliciously silky and smooth, and vegan cheeses are just as creamy and decadent as their dairy counterparts. You can even find an extensive variety of vegan meats that look and taste so much like the real thing that you can't tell the difference!

Veganism is a way of living that excludes the use of animal products and by-products in all aspects of life, including diet. Vegans avoid eating meat, dairy, eggs, honey, and other animal by-products such as lard, whey, and casein.

You might be wondering: "What do vegans eat?" I totally get it. It may seem as though vegan diets are limiting, considering how animal by-products sneak their way into so many processed foods, but I promise you there's plenty of scrumptious food to eat!

Today, the vegan food scene is exploding as more and more food giants produce and invest in plant-based foods to meet growing customer demand. At most major grocery stores, you'll find much more than just beans and tofu (although you're going to love those, too!). You'll see cold cases piled high with juicy vegan hot dogs, crispy chicken-free nuggets and fish-free fillets, "beefy" meatballs, succulent holiday roasts, smoky deli slices, and a wide variety of plant-based burgers that literally bleed when you cook them. Creamy vegan yogurts, decadent ice creams, and cheeses of all kinds are all also widely available.

Dining out is super easy, too. From the smallest towns in America to the biggest metropolises, yummy vegan food is everywhere.

It's truly never been easier—or tastier—to eat vegan.

So, what is vegan exactly? According to the Vegan Society, "Veganism is a way of living which seeks to exclude, as far as is possible and practicable, all forms of exploitation of, and cruelty to, animals for food, clothing, or any other purpose." Simply put, vegans do their best to avoid the use of animal products and by-products. This means choosing pleather over leather and veggie burgers over beef burgers as a way to save a cow's life, combat climate change, and reduce air, soil, and water pollution. It also means swapping traditional eggs for plant-based eggs as a way to stand up for mother hens.

Although some people choose to go vegan mainly to help animals, everyone's story, starting point, and motivations are different. Some people go vegan to save the planet, as raising animals for food is one of the leading causes of environmental degradation. I began my vegan journey to improve my personal health. And over the years, it's brought joy into every aspect of my life. And it brings me even more joy that you're here so we can learn and cook together.

The Difference between Vegetarians and Vegans

Think of vegan as the original vegetarian diet—consisting of whole fruits, vegetables, grains, and plant-based proteins such as legumes, nuts, and seeds as its primary staples. While all vegetarians—including lacto (dairy-consuming) vegetarians and ovo (egg-consuming) vegetarians—avoid eating meat, vegans eliminate all animal products and by-products from their diet.

The term "vegan" was coined in 1944 by Donald Watson, founder of the Vegan Society, to describe vegetarians who did not consume any animal products. However, evidence suggests the original use of the word *vegetarian* in the 1830s described a person who followed what is now considered a vegan diet. It wasn't until after the formation of the Vegetarian Society in 1847 that the vegetarian diet came to include dairy and eggs.

In recent years, new terms such as "flexitarian" and "reducitarian" have been coined. "Flexitarians" are part-time vegans or vegetarians. A "reducitarian" is an omnivore who actively works to reduce his or her intake of meat, dairy, and eggs.

No matter which type of plant-based eater you choose to be, every vegan meal you eat is a great step toward a happier and healthier future.

Why Go Vegan?

There are so many reasons people go vegan or shift toward plant-based diets. Some are motivated by environmental reasons, others do it to help animals, and a growing number of people go vegan to improve their health.

Vegan for the Planet

Many of tomorrow's leaders are choosing to eat vegan to reduce their carbon footprint.

Animal agriculture is one of the leading causes of climate change. According to the Food and Agriculture Organization of the United Nations, the meat industry is responsible for nearly 20 percent of global greenhouse gas emissions. Methane emissions from livestock and other agricultural practices are 84 times more potent than carbon dioxide. Steve Hamburg, chief scientist at the Environmental Defense Fund, states, "By emitting just a little bit of methane, mankind is greatly accelerating the rate of climatic change."

According to the Food and Agriculture Organization of the United Nations, another problem facing the environment is water pollution caused by animal agriculture. As the human population increases and the demand for meat continues to rise, factory farms now produce an estimated 500 million tons of manure each year, which is stored in massive cesspools or lagoons that often leak into waterways. This poses huge threats to both aquatic systems and human health.

Raising animals for food is also extremely resource intensive. Oxfam International, a relief organization that works to secure food for our exploding global population, encourages its members to reduce meat consumption, saying in a CNN piece, "It takes massive amounts of land, water, fertilizer, oil, and other resources to produce meat, significantly more than it requires to grow other nutritious and delicious kinds of food." Consider this from the US Geological Survey: It takes about 2,000 gallons of water to produce a single pound of beef compared to just 200 gallons of water to produce the same amount of beans, potatoes, or wheat.

Deforestation is another concern. As the demand for meat increases, so does the amount of land needed for animal factories and processing facilities. Animal agriculture, according to the Food and Agriculture Organization of the United Nations, is responsible for nearly a third of the earth's biodiversity loss, owing to the dangerous effects of deforestation.

Taking care of the planet is our moral obligation. Small dietary changes like swapping beef for a plant-based alternative can make a big difference for future generations.

Vegan for the Animals

Cows, pigs, chickens, and other animals raised for food are amazing beings that are capable of thinking, feeling, and displaying personalities, just like our beloved pets. That's why many people choose to eat vegan to spare these sentient beings suffering and harm.

Cows are intelligent and socially complex animals who are just as diverse as our own friends and families. Some are shy, some playful, and some just like to lounge all day. Cows are known to form strong bonds with their companions. They even mourn the deaths and losses of loved ones. On dairy factory farms, baby male calves are separated from their mothers at birth and shipped off to veal factories, where they will be castrated and dehorned without painkillers, because they are useless in the dairy industry. This separation causes mother cows endless fear and anxiety, yet they endure this repeated suffering owing to the forced impregnation that's standard in the dairy industry. All cows—whether raised for milk or meat—face a grim ending on their way to slaughter, where they are crammed together on trucks without food, water, or rest for the duration of the trip. The often multiple-day journey can cause cows to suffer heat strokes during extremely hot weather and freeze to death during extremely cold weather.

Pigs are curious, outgoing individuals that animal behaviorists consider to be smarter than our canine companions! And contrary to popular belief, they are very tidy animals who like to keep their living areas clean. In natural environments, pigs like to run around and play, sunbathe, and explore their surroundings. But on factory farms, pigs are confined to crowded warehouses where they never see sunlight or breathe fresh air. Like dairy cows, mother pigs are forcibly impregnated and spend most of their lives in tiny metal crates, where they are unable to turn around, lie down comfortably, or even nurture their newborn piglets. Being trapped in these tight confinement systems causes both physical and mental trauma to mother pigs.

Chickens are very social and inquisitive animals that are just as intelligent as dogs, cats, and even some primates. According to an article published in *Animal Cognition*, they even possess characteristics of self-awareness, such as self-control and assessment of their own position in the pecking order. In natural surroundings, chickens enjoy dustbathing, roosting in trees, scratching for food, and taking in the sun. Sadly, chickens are the most abused land animals on the planet.

Chickens raised for meat are called "broilers" by the meat industry. They spend their entire lives crammed in dark, filthy sheds. "Broiler" chickens are bred to grow so large so fast they often suffer heart attacks, organ failure, and painful, crippling leg disorders. Those birds who survive are crammed into cages and sent to slaughter at only six or seven weeks old.

Chickens raised for eggs are called "laying hens" by the egg industry. These mother hens are forced to spend their entire lives in stacks upon stacks of tiny wire cages among other hens, where they don't even have enough room to spread their wings. Because their living conditions are so cramped, hens get their beaks cut off so they won't peck each other out of frustration. When the hens are "spent"—too exhausted to produce enough eggs—they are often sent to slaughter to be used for cat or dog food. Like male calves in the dairy industry, baby male chicks are useless for the egg industry. And because they are not bred to produce excessive amounts of flesh, they are killed immediately.

Turkeys are very social birds that enjoy the company of others—including humans! They love having their feathers stroked and chirping along to music. In nature, turkeys spend their days dustbathing, building nests, foraging for food, and grooming themselves. They can fly at speeds of up to 55 miles per hour and run at speeds of up to 25 miles per hour. The natural life-span of a turkey can be up to ten years, but on factory farms, they are typically slaughtered at just four to six months of age. Like "broiler" chickens, turkeys in the meat industry are forced to spend their entire lives in dark, cramped sheds and are bred to grow so large and so fast that many become crippled under their own weight.

Fish, too, are social and intelligent beings with their own unique personalities. Macquarie University biologist Dr. Culum Brown, who is studying the evolution of cognition in fish, says, "Fish are more intelligent than they appear. In many areas, such as memory, their cognitive powers match or exceed those of 'higher' vertebrates including non-human primates." Like birds, many fish build nests to raise their finned families. And they protect themselves from predators by building hiding places to rest. Sadly, more fish are killed each year than all other animals combined. On fish factory farms, fish are crammed by the thousands in dirty ponds or crowded concrete tanks. Because there are no legal protections for fish, these amazing animals are often suffocated, skinned alive, or cut open and gutted while still fully conscious.

We can all save farm animals from a life of pain and suffering simply by leaving them off our plates.

CHAPTER TWO

The Health Benefits of a Vegan Diet

Research shows that diets rich in fruits, vegetables, whole grains, and plant-based proteins like legumes, nuts, and seeds are great for your overall health. People who eat a vegan diet lower their risk for heart disease, type 2 diabetes, obesity, and other chronic diseases.

Heart Health

Heart disease is the leading cause of death in the United States. The Centers for Disease Control and Prevention reports that in the United States, heart disease takes the life of one person every 37 seconds, totaling roughly 647,000 people per year. Eating habits play a key role in determining the risk of heart disease. And research reported by the Physicians Committee for Responsible Medicine shows that vegan diets don't just prevent heart disease, they can also reverse it.

A landmark study conducted by Dr. Dean Ornish and Dr. Caldwell Esselstyn, of the Cleveland Clinic, tested the effects of a plant-based diet on participants with moderate to severe heart disease. Within weeks, 90 percent of patients' chest pain diminished; after one month, blood flow to the heart improved; and after one year, even severely blocked arteries had reopened.

According to the Physicians Committee for Responsible Medicine, "Plant-based diets benefit heart health because they contain no dietary cholesterol, very little saturated fat, and abundant fiber. Meat, cheese, and eggs, on the other hand, are packed with cholesterol and saturated fat, which cause plaque buildup in the arteries, eventually leading to heart disease."

Because vegan diets are cholesterol-free and high in fiber and potassium, they can also help improve risk factors for heart disease, including high blood pressure, high cholesterol, inflammation, and atherosclerosis, a disease caused by the buildup of fatty plaque in artery walls.

Diabetes Prevention

According to the Centers for Disease Control and Prevention, more than 30 million Americans are living with type 2 diabetes, a chronic condition that affects the way the body metabolizes sugar. Type 2 diabetes is caused by insulin resistance, or when the pancreas is not able to produce enough insulin, which regulates the movement of sugar into the cells.

Being overweight is the main risk factor for type 2 diabetes, and complications could lead to heart disease, nerve damage, kidney damage, eye diseases such as glaucoma and cataracts, hearing impairment, and a laundry list of other preventable diseases. Type 2 diabetes, previously called "adult-onset diabetes," has become increasingly more prevalent in children owing to our childhood obesity crisis.

Vegan diets have been proven to manage, prevent, and even reverse type 2 diabetes. A 2003 study by the National Institutes of Health determined that a vegan diet controlled blood sugar three times more effectively than a traditional diabetes diet that limited calories and carbohydrates. Within weeks on the vegan diet, study participants lost weight, insulin sensitivity improved, and glycohemoglobin levels dropped.

Cancer Risk Reduction

Cancer is the second leading cause of death in the United States, and roughly a third of all cancer cases could be prevented with diet alone. Research suggests the key to fighting cancer is eating more fruits, vegetables, and legumes and little to no meat. The World Cancer Research Fund International and the American Institute for Cancer Research state, "Basing our diets around plant foods (like vegetables, fruits, whole grains, and beans), which contain fiber and other nutrients, can reduce our risk of cancer."

The reason? Phytochemicals, exclusively produced by plants (*phyto* means "plant"), have an abundance of cancer-fighting compounds that help stop the formation of potential cancer-causing substances (carcinogens), and help stop carcinogens from attacking cells.

Some of the most powerful phytochemicals are beta-carotene (in carrots, sweet potatoes, and winter squashes), polyphenols (in berries, beans, and dark chocolate), and isothiocyanates (in cruciferous vegetables like Brussels sprouts, kale, collard greens, broccoli, and cauliflower).

The Physicians Committee for Responsible Medicine states, "Avoiding animal products and high-fat foods and eating plant-based foods can lower the risk of developing certain types of cancer," showing yet again that plant-based diets may help prevent cancer by boosting fiber. Fiber consumption removes waste from the digestive system, which helps prevent colorectal cancer. It also helps remove excess hormones that could lead to breast and prostate cancer.

Weight Management

Whether it's chosen to lose weight or maintain a healthy weight, a healthy vegan diet can help you achieve your goals.

For many Americans, weight management is more than a cosmetic issue. The Centers for Disease Control and Prevention reports that obesity rates in the United States have reached an all-time high—affecting more than 40 percent of US adults and 18 percent of children and teens. Obesity is associated with type 2 diabetes, heart disease, high blood pressure, stroke, fatty liver disease, sleep apnea, arthritis, gallbladder disease, and other chronic, preventable diseases.

Nutrition experts worldwide agree that replacing high-fat foods with fruits, vegetables, whole grains, and legumes naturally reduces calorie intake and can lead to weight loss—even without exercise. Vegan diets can help people lose weight because they are packed with fiber, which helps you feel satiated without adding calories.

EDDIE'S STORY

I grew up in far South Texas, a region plagued by childhood obesity, diabetes, and heart disease. Like many of my childhood peers, I struggled with serious weight problems from an early age, maxing out at a whopping 310 pounds by the time I was 21 years old. I was prediabetic, depressed, and constantly getting injured because I simply could not support my own weight. I had read study after study on the positive effects vegan diets had on obesity-related illnesses, so I decided to try it. After five years of trial and error, I was able to naturally lose 150 pounds and reverse my declining health. Today, when I see images of "broiler" chickens and turkeys crippled under their own weight on factory farms, it brings tears to my eyes. The meat industry breeds these majestic birds to grow so unnaturally large that they suffer from some of the same health conditions obese people suffer, including heart attacks, organ failure, and crippling leg disorders. A vegan diet may have saved my life, but it also opened my heart to the lives of all sentient beings.

Vegan Nutrition

Many health benefits are associated with vegan diets—from reducing the risk of heart disease and certain cancers to shedding pounds and reversing type 2 diabetes. When you start any new diet, however, it's important to learn some nutrition basics. Eating a variety of fruits, vegetables, whole grains, and plant-based proteins like legumes, nuts, and seeds is a great foundation for a healthy vegan diet. But for optimum health, you'll want to pay attention to some key nutrients.

Calcium

Calcium is vital for optimum bone health. The heart, muscles, and nerves also need calcium to function properly. The recommended daily allowance (RDA) from the National Institutes of Health for calcium is 1,000 mg for adults and 1,200 mg for older adults (71 years and older).

Good sources of vegan calcium include soy foods like edamame, tempeh, and tofu; legumes like beans, chickpeas, and lentils; and certain nuts like almonds, macadamia nuts, and walnuts. Calcium-rich vegetables include broccoli, Brussels sprouts, cabbage, kale, and okra. Plant-based milks are also often fortified with around 300 mg of calcium per cup.

Iron

Iron is an important nutrient that helps with many vital body functions, including general energy and focus, digestion, and body temperature regulation. The National Institutes of Health recommends 8 mg daily for adult men, 18 mg daily for women, 28 mg daily for pregnant women, and 9 mg daily for lactating women.

Legumes, whole grains, nuts, seeds, and leafy greens are all rich in iron. However, it's important to pair iron-rich foods with foods high in vitamin C to maximize absorption. Some good sources of iron include beans, cashews, chia seeds, chickpeas, hemp seeds, kale, lentils, pumpkin seeds, quinoa, and tofu. Pair these foods with vitamin C–rich foods like bell peppers, broccoli, Brussels sprouts, cabbage, and citrus fruits.

Omega-3 Fatty Acids

Omega-3 fatty acids are essential for our immune system, brain health, nerves, and eyes. The three main omega-3 fatty acids are alpha-linolenic acid (ALA), eicosapentaenoic acid (EPA), and docosahexaenoic acid (DHA). Good vegan sources of ALA include chia seeds, ground flaxseed, hemp seeds, and walnuts. EPA and DHA sources include sea vegetables like chlorella, nori seaweed, and spirulina. Vegan EPA/DHA supplements made from microalgae (where fish get their omega-3s) are also recommended by health experts.

Vitamin B_{12}

It's vital for anyone following a vegan diet to include a reliable source of vitamin B_{12}, which is responsible for healthy functioning of the brain and nervous system, as well as formation of red blood cells. The National Institutes of Health recommends 2.4 mcg for adults, 2.6 mcg for pregnant women, and 2.8 mcg for lactating women daily.

Vegan sources of vitamin B_{12} include fortified foods like plant-based milks, cereals, nutritional yeast, and some plant-based meats. Experts suggest two servings per day of foods fortified with 2 to 3.5 mcg of vitamin B_{12} each. A daily supplement providing 25 to 100 mcg of vitamin B_{12}, or 1,000 mcg two times a week, is also recommended.

Vitamin D

The human body has evolved to produce vitamin D naturally when it's directly exposed to sunlight, but studies show that some environmental factors can impact the body's ability to produce sufficient amounts. Our bodies need vitamin D for regulating the absorption of calcium and phosphorus and for facilitating normal immune system function. Vitamin D deficiency can result in bone abnormalities, such as soft bones (osteomalacia) or fragile bones (osteoporosis).

For most adults, 10 to 20 minutes daily of direct sunlight exposure is enough for the body to produce sufficient vitamin D. When not possible, a vitamin D supplement is recommended. When choosing a supplement, look for vitamins labeled "vegetarian" or "vegan." Vitamin D_2 is almost always vegan friendly.

Vitamin D_3, the most common form of vitamin D, is almost always derived from animal sources. However, there are a few vitamin D_3 supplements on the market made from the plant source lichen.

Zinc

Zinc is essential for a healthy immune system and metabolic function. The National Institutes of Health recommends 11 mg for adult men, 8 mg for adult women, 11 mg for pregnant women, and 12 mg for lactating women daily.

Good vegan sources of zinc include cashews, chia seeds, hemp seeds, pumpkin seeds, tofu, walnuts, and legumes like beans, chickpeas, and lentils.

THE PROTEIN MYTH

Vegans are asked all the time: "Where do you get your protein?" The truth is if you're eating a well-balanced vegan diet and sufficient calories, you're likely getting enough protein. Based on the recommended daily allowance (0.8 gram per kilogram [0.36 gram per pound] of body weight), the average 150-pound person needs only 54 grams.

It's easy to meet that recommendation on a vegan diet. Tofu, seitan (wheat meat), tempeh, and legumes are all great sources of vegan protein. In fact, a single cup of seitan provides more than a full day's recommended amount of protein for a 150-pound person. Other delicious protein-rich vegan foods include nuts, seeds, and plant-based meats. Even vegan athletes and bodybuilders, who try to consume more protein when training, can get enough protein on a vegan diet. Look at these protein powerhouses:

1 cup seitan = 63 g protein

1 cup tempeh = 41 g protein

1 cup tofu = 20 g protein

1 cup lentils = 18 g protein

1 cup black beans = 15 g protein

1 cup quinoa = 9 g protein

¼ cup nutritional yeast = 8 g protein

Wild Rice and Lentil Stuffed Acorn Squash, page 150

CHAPTER THREE

Your Vegan Kitchen and Meal Plan

The key to succeeding at any new meal plan is having a well-stocked kitchen. With some basic pantry items and kitchen essentials, you'll be prepared to put together a vegan meal in minutes.

Vegan Staples

You likely have many of the staples we'll use over the next 30 days—such as herbs, spices, grains, and pastas—but there are a few special items you'll want on hand to help your vegan kitchen run seamlessly.

Beans, Beans, and More Beans!

All the beans I call for in this book can be swapped out for any other so as to mix things up. The basic legumes to keep on hand are black beans (also known as turtle beans), chickpeas (also known as garbanzo beans), lentils, pinto beans, and red beans or kidney beans. Stock up on both dried and canned or packaged beans.

Nuts and Seeds

Stock your pantry with an assortment of nuts and seeds. We'll use cashews frequently to make decadent sauces such as Cashew Hollandaise (page 135). Macadamia nuts are the base of Crostini with Macadamia Ricotta, Strawberries, and Basil (page 110). Walnuts, pine nuts, pumpkin seeds, hemp seeds, flaxseed, and chia seeds enhance multiple dishes to increase nutritional value. Peanuts are introduced in Napa Cabbage Salad (page 72). Almonds, pistachios, and sunflower seeds are nice snacks.

Specialty Grains—or Are They Seeds?

Amaranth and quinoa are ancient "super" seeds often mislabeled as grains because they have some of the same uses and characteristics. These two seed siblings are more closely related to beets than to any grain. And they're packed with protein, fiber, amino acids, and important micronutrients.

Stocks and Broths

Vegan-friendly stocks and broths can be found at most grocery stores in cubed, jarred concentrated, and ready-to-use liquid forms. My favorite brand is Better Than Bouillon, which makes several vegan-friendly concentrates. Or look for Pacific Foods' vegetable broth, Imagine's vegetarian no-chicken broth, or Swanson's 100 percent natural organic vegetable broth.

Moo-ve Over, Dairy!

You'll be surprised to learn how easy it is to trade in your old dairy products for the wide array of vegan alternatives available at your local grocer.

Vegan Butter

Vegan butters come in a variety of styles—from cultured cashew butters for spreading on toast to olive oil-based buttery sticks for baking. My personal favorite is Miyoko's Creamery European Style Cultured Vegan Butter, which melts, browns, bakes, and spreads just like traditional dairy butter. If you can't find Miyoko's Creamery brand, consider one of these great alternatives: Earth Balance, Country Crock's plant butter, or I Can't Believe It's Not Butter! brand's It's Vegan.

Vegan Cheese

Most grocery stores carry an assortment of delicious vegan cheeses. You can find them in slices, shreds, crumbles, blocks, and tubs in an array of flavors. Some of my favorites include Follow Your Heart's Dairy-Free Cheddar Shreds, Violife's smoked provolone and Just like Parmesan wedge, Miyoko's Creamery Fresh Vegan Mozzarella, and Kite Hill's almond milk cream cheese spread. In this book, we'll also make our own basic cheeses.

Vegan Sour Cream

Vegan sour cream is an essential topper for a number of dishes in this book. My vegan sour cream is Cashew Cream (page 139). For anyone looking for a nut-free alternative, try Tofutti Better Than Sour Cream, Good Karma's plant-based sour cream, and WayFare's dairy-free sour cream.

Vegan Milks

At most grocery stores these days you'll find a plethora of milks made from nuts, seeds, legumes, and grains. In addition, you can also find banana milk, coconut milk, flax milk, hemp milk, pea milk, and rice milk.

ALMOND MILK

Almond milk is an easy-to-find, low-fat choice that's high in vitamin E, selenium, iron, and potassium. It comes in a variety of styles, including unsweetened, original, vanilla, unsweetened vanilla, and chocolate.

CASHEW MILK

Cashew milk is a great source of antioxidants and fiber. Its extra-creamy consistency makes it perfect for coffee drinks.

OAT MILK

Oat milk is becoming ever more popular for its versatility and ability to mimic dairy milk in frothy beverages. It's a great alternative to cashew milk for folks with nut allergies.

SOYMILK

Naturally high in protein, soymilk is still the most widely available vegan milk. Like almond milk, it comes in a variety of styles, such as unsweetened, original, vanilla, unsweetened vanilla, chocolate, and strawberry, and even as an eggnog alternative during the holiday season.

Nutritional Yeast

Nutritional yeast, also called nooch, is a wonderfully versatile condiment with a somewhat nutty, cheesy flavor. Packed with protein, folic acid, and vitamin B_{12}, nutritional yeast adds a little cheesiness to sauces and seasonings and is a flavor enhancer. Nutritional yeast can be found in the natural foods aisle of well-stocked grocery stores, online, or at your local health food or vitamin store.

Creamy Vegan Salad Dressings

We'll make a few yummy dressings, such as Cashew Caesar Dressing (page 128), Balsamic Reduction (page 137), and a Vinaigrette Trio (page 126), but you might want to stock a few store-bought dressings for variety. A few of my favorites are Annie's Goddess Dressing, Daiya's Creamy Italian and Homestyle Ranch, and Follow Your Heart's Vegan Thousand Island and Bleu Cheese.

Cluck-Free Kitchen

Whether you're in the mood for a fluffy omelet or a three-tiered cake, I promise you there's no need for chicks in this vegan kitchen! Here are my favorite vegan egg alternatives.

Aquafaba

Aquafaba is the water or brine from cooked or canned chickpeas that most people drain and toss. But you shouldn't. It's the key ingredient in Aquafaba Mayo (page 141) used in Classic Chick-Free Salad (page 77). This magical ingredient has risen to fame over the past few years because of its astonishing ability to transform into puffy meringue, whipped cream, sweet macarons, and other sweet treats like our Aquafaba Mint-Chocolate Mousse (page 173). Aquafaba has also become a favorite in the mixology world for making "eggy" cocktails like the whisky sour, gin fizz, and clover club.

Flax Meal

Ground flaxseed, also known as flax meal, isn't just a good source of omega-3s; it also makes a great alternative for eggs as a binding agent. Combine 1 tablespoon flax meal with 3 tablespoons water for the equivalent of 1 egg. Use "flax eggs" in place of traditional eggs for pancakes, waffles, and any baked goods.

Tofu

Tofu is a versatile soy-based protein that easily absorbs any flavor you add to it.

Other Vegan Egg Replacers

Bob's Red Mill and Ener-G both make powdered egg replacers that work well for baking.

Follow Your Heart makes a powdered egg alternative called VeganEgg that quickly comes together with a little vegan butter and water. It can be sautéed with any assortment of veggies for a fulfilling breakfast.

JUST Egg is a new liquid egg alternative made entirely from plants that whips up into fluffy omelets, quiches, frittatas, and more. You can find it at most health food stores, well-stocked grocery stores, and even some Walmart stores.

HELPFUL EQUIPMENT

All recipes in this book can be made easily with standard kitchen equipment, but a few extra tools and gadgets will make things easier—and quicker!

Tofu Press: To prep for steaks and kabobs, tofu needs to be pressed to remove excess water. One common method is to sandwich the tofu block between porous kitchen towels and place the flat side of a heavy pan (such as an iron skillet) on top of the tofu block. The easier method is to use a tofu press, which is made to press the water out of tofu with very little mess. Tofu presses can be purchased online and at select health food stores.

High-Speed Blender: For the creamiest sauces, dressings, and bisques, I recommend using a high-speed blender. There are great options on the market for any budget—from the economy Oster Versa to the top-of-the-line Vitamix Pro or Blendtec.

Chef's Knife: Nothing super fancy required here—just a knife that's sharp and durable. For beginners in the kitchen, I recommend Victorinox's Fibrox Pro 8-inch chef's knife, which retails for $30 to $40.

Electric Pressure Cooker: An electric pressure cooker can be a real time-saver in the kitchen. On meal prep days, it's the one machine I have working all day to cook the many pounds of legumes and grains we'll eat all week. Basic electric pressure cookers can be purchased for about $50. High-end Wi-Fi-enabled cookers start at around $150.

Meet Your New Meat

With the abundance of meat alternatives on the market, you can skip the bloody butcher counter and still make all your favorite meaty meals!

Cauliflower

Battered and baked, cauliflower makes a great stand-in for fish in our Crispy Cauliflower Po' Boys (page 100) and for chicken in our Baked Barbecue Cauliflower Wings (page 115).

Chickpeas

Chickpeas are a versatile legume that can be enjoyed hot or cold. We'll use chickpeas as the base for Classic Chick-Free Salad (page 77). For a main course, chickpeas simmer in a curried tomato and onion sauce for our Easy Chana Masala (page 156).

Jackfruit

Young jackfruit, also called "green jackfruit," is a species of fruit in the fig family that has become a global phenomenon. Its texture resembles shredded meat and it easily absorbs any seasoning you add to it. Young jackfruit is typically sold in the United States in canned and vacuum-sealed forms. You can find it in the natural foods aisle of well-stocked grocery stores, online, or at your local health food store. High in fiber and potassium, jackfruit is a fat-free, low-calorie food, making it the perfect choice for Jackfruit Barbecue Sandwiches (page 99).

Mushrooms

Cooking mushrooms brings out their deep, rich umami flavor, making them one of the earth's yummiest natural meat alternatives. There are so many varieties to choose from—all with their unique flavor characteristics. We'll use the husky portobello mushroom for our Portobello Steak and Tofu Eggs with Oven Home Fries (page 64) and Seared Portobello Fajitas (page 153). The humble white button mushroom takes the spotlight in Mushroom-Lentil Shepherd's Pie (page 160). And we'll explore more exotic mushrooms in Herbed Oyster Mushroom White Cream Flatbread (page 158) and Wild Mushroom and Vegetable Fried Rice (page 155).

Tempeh

Tempeh is a protein-packed fermented soy product with a delightfully nutty taste. Just 1 cup of tempeh contains 41 grams of plant protein. Tempeh can be found near the other vegan meats in the produce section of most major grocery stores. We'll use this protein staple for Tempeh Bacon (page 120) and a number of dishes, including Tempeh BLTs (page 103).

Tofu

An excellent source of amino acids, iron, calcium, and other micronutrients, tofu is a popular protein made from soybeans. It's one of the first processed foods known to humans and continues to demonstrate its remarkable versatility. We use tofu as an alternative to eggs, but tofu also steps in for meat. We'll marinate and grill tofu for Grilled Tofu and Veggie Kabobs with Chimichurri Sauce (page 116) and sear it for savory Tofu Chops with Caramelized Apple and Onion (page 151). You can find tofu near the other vegan meats in the produce section of most grocery stores.

Vital Wheat Gluten

Vital wheat gluten is the natural protein extracted from wheat. It's the main ingredient for the popular meat substitute seitan. We'll blend vital wheat gluten with beans and a variety of herbs and spices to craft Seitan Sausage 3 Ways (page 106). These plant-based links can be enjoyed as midday snacks or in dishes like Italian Seitan Sausage Hoagies (page 96), Spanish Chorizo and Vegetable Paella (page 164), and Seitan Sausage Jambalaya (page 159). Vital wheat gluten can be found in the baking aisle of any health food store and most well-stocked grocery stores.

READING FOOD LABELS

When shopping for groceries, try to purchase packaged items that display the "Certified Vegan" label. But most brands choose not to pay the annual licensing fee required to display the logo, so you'll want to become a stealth label reader.

Check ingredients carefully when buying staples such as refried beans to make sure they don't contain lard, a fat obtained by rendering fatty pork. Lard is also a common ingredient in flour tortillas and other flatbreads.

Being labeled "nondairy" doesn't mean creamers and whipped toppings are vegan or even totally dairy-free. They likely contain casein, a milk protein.

Look for breads and pastas that don't contain eggs or whey, a by-product of milk. Whey is often also found in vegetable margarines, baking mixes, and even some vegetarian meats. A few vegetarian meats on the market also contain eggs, so watch out.

Many whole wheat and whole-grain breads also contain honey, which many vegans avoid as a way to protect honeybees and their homes. Honey often sneaks into teas, natural cereals, and snack bars and trail mixes, too.

Gelatin comes from animal bones and hooves and is a common ingredient in candies, vitamin capsules, and sweet cereals. Gelatin-free vitamins will always display the word *vegetarian* on the label.

Also look for carmine in candies, juices, and other red-tinted foods. Carmine—also known as "cochineal" or "natural red 4"—is a ruby-red dye produced from insects.

Animal by-products sneak their way into everything from food to fashion to personal hygiene and skin-care products. For a full list of ingredients to watch out for, visit PETA.org/living/food/animal-ingredients-list.

Dining Out

Eating out today as a vegan is easier and more delicious than ever!

For a vegan burger fix, stop by any BurgerFi, Burger King, Carl's Jr., Cheesecake Factory, Denny's, Habit Burger Grill, Houston's, Johnny Rockets, Red Robin, Ruby Tuesday, Shake Shack, TGI Fridays, or White Castle.

Craving vegan Mexican food? Try the sofritas at Chipotle, the Impossible Fajita Bowl at Qdoba, or the Beyond Meat bowl at Freebirds World Burrito. Del Taco, El Pollo Loco, On the Border Mexican Grill and Cantina, Pancheros Mexican Grill, and Taco Bell all carry vegan options, too.

Even pizza's on the menu! Blaze Pizza, PizzaRev, zpizza, Mellow Mushroom, and Yard House offer vegan meat and cheese options. In addition to pizzas, Yard House has an entire selection of vegan dishes featuring Gardein products, including my personal favorite, the Gardein Chicken Bowl.

Olive Garden has an assortment of vegan-friendly pastas, including angel hair, cavatappi, fettuccine, rigatoni, small shells, spaghetti, and whole wheat linguine, which can be topped with the vegan marinara or kid's tomato sauce. And you'll be delighted to know their minestrone and breadsticks are also vegan.

P. F. Chang's Pei Wei Asian Diner and Kona Grill are vegan friendly. In fact, most Asian restaurants are very accommodating to vegans.

Baskin-Robbins, Ben & Jerry's, Pressed Juicery, Red Mango, and TCBY are your go-to places for a vegan-friendly frozen treat.

Of course, there are many amazing 100 percent vegan restaurants across the country. To find one near you, check out HappyCow.net.

Meal Plan by Lauren Pitts, MA, RD

Welcome to plant-based eating! Whether you are a full-time plant eater or just dipping your toe in the water for the first time (don't worry, plants don't bite), we are happy you are here and we have amazing recipes for you to try.

As a registered dietitian, I have dedicated my career to plant-based nutrition as a comprehensive approach to improving our health, the planet, and the animals we share it with. My experience includes individual client counseling, working alongside brilliant chefs, and transforming menus of some of the largest food-service companies in the world. What I've learned is no matter how big or small the change is that you are striving to make, it can be overwhelming, especially when changing food-based behaviors. Food choices are personal and often stem from family, social, emotional, and even ethical sentiments. The bottom line is that people want delicious, comforting foods they can feel good about. Food that helps you live longer, fight off chronic disease, and boost your mood, and that tastes good—all the while showing kindness to the world around us. The great news is that chefs around the globe are taking an interest in plant-forward cuisine and getting creative in the kitchen, so you can still enjoy your favorite dishes while reaping the many benefits of eating plant-based.

By the time you reach this chapter, I am sure you're eager to try the delectable, nutritionally balanced recipes created by Chef Eddie Garza.

I am excited to offer this 30-day meal plan and corresponding grocery lists to kick off your plant-based lifestyle. The meal plan is your quick guide to a professionally curated menu for two that includes breakfast, lunch, dinner, snacks, and desserts with leftovers for those times you don't feel like cooking.

This plan is designed to be varied and satiating, so you will never go hungry. It's packed with plant proteins such as beans, tofu, nuts, and whole grains with a hefty helping of fiber, leaving you feeling satisfied yet energized.

For even more convenience, we include four weekly shopping lists that break down this four-week plan into bite-sized pieces so you do not feel overwhelmed at the grocery store. The shopping lists will help ensure you have all the essentials you need and save money by not overstocking on unnecessary items. Be sure to check your pantry before you go shopping the first time.

Now, it's time to have fun exploring these new foods and a plant-based lifestyle. I hope these resources are helpful and empower you to live a healthier life and achieve your goals through the power of food.

WEEK 1	MONDAY	TUESDAY	WEDNESDAY
BREAKFAST	Avocado Toast-adas	Avocado Toast-adas (*leftovers*)	Tofu Egg Sandwiches
LUNCH	Jackfruit Barbecue Sandwiches	Seitan Sausage Jambalaya (*leftovers*)	Jackfruit Barbecue Sandwiches (*leftovers*)
DINNER	Seitan Sausage Jambalaya	Sweet Potato and Shiitake Mushroom Risotto	Tofu Chops with Caramelized Apple and Onion
SNACK OR DESSERT	Mango Shiitake Ceviche	Texas-Style Pineapple-Mango Cobbler	Crostini with Macadamia Ricotta, Strawberries, and Basil; Balsamic Reduction

THURSDAY	FRIDAY	SATURDAY	SUNDAY
Tofu Egg Sandwiches (*leftovers*)	Berry Superfood Smoothie Bowls	Berry Superfood Smoothie Bowls (*leftovers*)	Tofu Eggs Benedict with Tempeh Bacon, Wilted Spinach, and Cashew Hollandaise
Sweet Potato and Shiitake Mushroom Risotto (*leftovers*)	Tex-Mex Taco Salad	Macadamia-Cashew Carbonara with Tempeh Bacon (*leftovers*)	Spicy Bean Tamales (*leftovers*)
Macadamia-Cashew Carbonara with Tempeh Bacon	Wild Rice and Lentil Stuffed Acorn Squash	Spicy Bean Tamales	Wild Rice and Lentil Stuffed Acorn Squash (*leftovers*)
—	Crostini with Macadamia Ricotta, Strawberries, and Basil; Balsamic Reduction (*leftovers*)	—	Texas-Style Pineapple Mango Cobbler (*leftovers*)

WEEK 2	MONDAY	TUESDAY	WEDNESDAY
BREAKFAST	Easy Overnight Oats	Tofu Egg Sandwiches; Tempeh Bacon	Blueberry Oatmeal with Walnuts, Banana, and Coconut
LUNCH	Portobello Steak and Chimichurri Sandwiches	Gallo Pinto; Pan-Sautéed Sweet Plantains (*leftovers*)	Pasta Bolognese; Basil Pesto (*leftovers*)
DINNER	Gallo Pinto; Pan-Sautéed Sweet Plantains	Pasta Bolognese; Basil Pesto	Herbed Oyster Mushroom White Cream Flatbread
SNACK OR DESSERT	Baked Barbecue Cauliflower Wings	Aquafaba Mint-Chocolate Mousse	Baked Barbecue Cauliflower Wings (*leftovers*)

THURSDAY	FRIDAY	SATURDAY	SUNDAY
Tofu Egg Sandwiches; Tempeh Bacon (*leftovers*)	Blueberry Oatmeal with Walnuts, Banana, and Coconut (*leftovers*)	Avocado Toast-adas	Tofu Eggs Benedict with Tempeh Bacon, Wilted Spinach, and Cashew Hollandaise
Lentil Sloppy Joes	Lentil Sloppy Joes (*leftovers*)	Caribbean Jerk Tempeh Bowls (*leftovers*)	Avocado Toast-adas (*leftovers*)
Spanish Chorizo and Vegetable Paella	Caribbean Jerk Tempeh Bowls	Loaded English Jacket Potatoes	Spanish Chorizo and Vegetable Paella (*leftovers*)
Baked Barbecue Cauliflower Wings (*leftovers*)	Aquafaba Mint-Chocolate Mousse (*leftovers*)	—	Watermelon, Cucumber, and Mint Salad

WEEK 3	MONDAY	TUESDAY	WEDNESDAY
BREAKFAST	Quinoa-Amaranth Porridge with Dried Cranberries and Pumpkin Seeds	Portobello Steak and Tofu Eggs with Oven Home Fries	Quinoa-Amaranth Porridge with Dried Cranberries and Pumpkin Seeds (*leftovers*)
LUNCH	Crispy Cauliflower Po' Boys	Easy Chana Masala (*leftovers*)	Crispy Cauliflower Po' Boys (*leftovers*)
DINNER	Easy Chana Masala	Mushroom-Lentil Shepherd's Pie	Portobello-Pineapple Poke Bowls
SNACK OR DESSERT	—	Peanut Butter, Chocolate, and Banana Milk Shake	—

THURSDAY	FRIDAY	SATURDAY	SUNDAY
Tex-Mex Migas; Restaurant-Style Chunky Red Salsa	Portobello Steak and Tofu Eggs with Oven Home Fries (*leftovers*)	Tex-Mex Migas; Restaurant-Style Chunky Red Salsa (*leftovers*)	Tofu Eggs Benedict with Tempeh Bacon, Wilted Spinach, and Cashew Hollandaise
Portobello-Pineapple Poke Bowls (*leftovers*)	Mushroom Lentil Shepherd's Pie (*leftovers*)	Seared Oyster Mushroom Tortas	Tex-Mex Tortilla Soup (*leftovers*)
Seitan Chorizo Tacos	Tex-Mex Tortilla Soup	Southwestern Black Bean and Quinoa Bowls	Seitan Chorizo Tacos (*leftovers*)
Chopped Fall Salad with Herbs	Peanut Butter, Chocolate, and Banana Milk Shake (*leftovers*)	Chopped Fall Salad with Herbs (*leftovers*)	—

WEEK 4	MONDAY	TUESDAY	WEDNESDAY	THURSDAY
BREAKFAST	Berry Superfood Smoothie Bowls	Tex-Mex Migas; Restaurant-Style Chunky Red Salsa	Berry Superfood Smoothie Bowls (*leftovers*)	Easy Overnight Oats
LUNCH	Seared Oyster Mushroom Tortas (*leftovers*)	Easy Three-Bean Chili; topped with Cashew Cream (*leftovers*)	Classic Chick-Free Salad; Aquafaba Mayo	Butternut Squash Mac and Cheese (*leftovers*)
DINNER	Easy Three-Bean Chili; topped with Cashew Cream	Seared Portobello Fajitas; Spanish Rice; Refried Pintos	Butternut Squash Mac and Cheese	Seared Portobello Fajitas; Spanish Rice; Refried Pintos (*leftovers*)
SNACK OR DESSERT	Spiced Sweet Potato Cheesecake	—	Spiced Sweet Potato Cheesecake (*leftovers*)	Italian-Herbed Roasted Chickpeas

FRIDAY	SATURDAY	SUNDAY	MONDAY	TUESDAY
Tex-Mex Migas; Restaurant-Style Chunky Red Salsa (*leftovers*)	Blueberry Oatmeal with Walnuts, Banana, and Coconut	Tofu Eggs Benedict with Tempeh Bacon, Wilted Spinach, and Cashew Hollandaise	Blueberry Oatmeal with Walnuts, Banana, and Coconut (*leftovers*)	Tofu Eggs Benedict with Tempeh Bacon, Wilted Spinach, and Cashew Hollandaise (*leftovers*)
Classic Chick-Free Salad; Aquafaba Mayo (*leftovers*)	Tempeh BLTs	Tropical Quinoa Salad	French Onion Soup (*leftovers*); Roasted Beet Salad with Baby Arugula and Macadamia Ricotta	Italian Seitan Sausage Hoagies (*leftovers*)
Wild Mushroom and Vegetable Fried Rice	French Onion Soup	Italian Seitan Sausage Hoagies	Caribbean Island Burgers with Mango Relish	Wild Mushroom and Vegetable Fried Rice (*leftovers*)
Spiced Sweet Potato Cheesecake (*leftovers*)	Caesar Salad with Italian-Herbed Roasted Chickpeas; Tempeh Bacon	Caesar Salad with Italian-Herbed Roasted Chickpeas; Tempeh Bacon (*leftovers*)	—	—

Shopping Lists

The shopping lists tell you everything you'll need to make each week's set of meals. The lists were created with at least some store-bought items, such as vegan mayo, in mind, though the book includes recipes to make your own from scratch if you'd prefer. You may already have quite a bit of what you need to get started. Be sure to check the spices chart below for an overview of what you'll need for the month, and read the Check Before You Shop section for each week, too! If the shopping lists feel long, remember that you're cooking with nutritious, fresh ingredients that will be used up each week.

SPICES, DRIED HERBS, EXTRACTS, AND OTHER FLAVORINGS

With these recipes, you'll be building flavors and cooking with a variety of spices. This chart lays out which spices and dried herbs you'll be using each week so you can plan ahead.

	Week 1	Week 2	Week 3	Week 4
allspice, ground		X		
black pepper, ground	X	X	X	X
cayenne	X	X		X
dark chili powder	X		X	X
cinnamon, ground	X			X
cloves, ground				X
coriander, ground			X	
cream of tartar		X		X

	Week 1	Week 2	Week 3	Week 4
cumin, ground		X	X	X
fennel seeds				X
garam masala spice blend			X	
garlic powder	X	X	X	X
ginger, ground				X
herbes de Provence dried herb blend	X		X	
Himalayan black salt	X	X	X	X
nutmeg, ground				X
onion powder	X	X	X	X
oregano, dried	X	X	X	X
paprika, smoked paprika, sweet		X	X	X
peppermint extract		X		
red pepper flakes		X		
rosemary, dried		X		X
sage, ground	X	X		X
salt	X	X	X	X
thyme, dried	X	X		X
turmeric, ground	X	X	X	X
vanilla extract	X	X	X	X
white pepper, ground	X	X	X	X

WEEK 1

CHECK BEFORE YOU SHOP

Agave nectar
All-purpose flour
Baking powder
Liquid smoke
Nutritional yeast
Olive oil
Soy sauce
Sugar, granulated
Toasted sesame oil
Truffle oil
Vegan mayonnaise
Vegetable oil
Vegetable oil spray
Vinegar, apple cider
Vinegar, balsamic
Vinegar, red wine
Wine, dry red
Wine, dry white

PANTRY SHOPPING LIST

Barbecue sauce, bottled (1 small)
Beans, black, canned (two 15-ounce cans)
Bread: burger buns, vegan (4)
Bread: English muffins (6)
Bread: French baguette (¼ loaf)
Cashews, raw, unsalted (4 cups)
Chia seeds (2 tablespoons)
Coconut flakes, unsweetened (¼ cup)
Coconut milk, unsweetened, full-fat, canned (½ cup)
Corn chips, bag (4 ounces)
Corn husks, large (8)
Corn masa flour (1½ cups)
Dates, pitted (2 or 3)
Dill pickle, sliced, jarred (handful)
Hemp seeds (2 tablespoons)
Jackfruit, canned (14 ounces)
Lentils, raw (1½ cups)
Linguine, dried (1 pound)
Macadamia nuts, raw, unsalted (1 cup)
Pumpkin seeds (½ cup)
Refried beans, vegan, canned (15 ounces)
Rice, arborio (1 cup)
Rice, long-grain white (2 cups)
Rice, wild (or brown or quinoa) (½ cup)
Rolled oats, old-fashioned (¾ cup)
Sweet potato puree, canned (1 cup)
Tomato sauce, canned (1 tablespoon)
Tomatoes, diced with juice, canned (28 ounces)
Tostadas, in box (8)
Vegetable broth (7 cups)
Walnut pieces (½ cup)

PRODUCE AND PERISHABLES SHOPPING LIST

Acorn squash (2 medium)
Almond milk, unsweetened (1 cup)
American cheese, vegan (4 slices)
Andouille sausage, vegan (2 links)
Apple, green (1 medium)
Avocado, Hass (4)
Bananas, ripe (2 medium)
Bell pepper, green (1 medium)
Bell pepper, red (½ medium)
Blackberries (½ cup)
Blueberries (1½ cups)
Button mushrooms (½ cup)
Celery (2 stalks)
Cheddar (or pepper Jack) cheese, vegan (½ cup shredded)
Cherry tomatoes (1 cup)
Corn chips (4 ounces)
Corn on the cob (2 ears)
Garlic (4 cloves)
Herbs, fresh: basil, chives, cilantro, flat-leaf parsley, sage (1 small bunch each)
Jalapeño pepper (1 medium)
Lemon (1)
Limes (8)
Mangos (3 large)
Oat milk, unsweetened (1½ cups)
Onion, red (1 medium)
Onion, yellow (4 medium)
Parmesan cheese, vegan (½ cup grated)
Pineapple, fresh (2 cups diced)
Raspberries (½ cup)
Red salsa, fresh (½ cup)
Romaine lettuce (1 head)
Scallions (1 bunch of 5)
Shiitake mushrooms (3 cups diced)
Spinach, baby (1 cup)
Strawberries (½ pint)
Tempeh (three 8-ounce packages)
Tofu, extra-firm (three 16-ounce packages)
Tofurky kielbasa (4 links)
Vegan butter (8 ounces)

PREP TIPS

- When making Fried Tofu Eggs with Tofu Egg Sandwiches, double the recipe for Tofu Eggs Benedict later in the week.
- When making Tempeh Bacon for Cashew Carbonara, double the recipe for Tofu Eggs Benedict later in the week.
- Use leftover Cashew Cream from Cashew Carbonara for Tex-Mex Taco Salad and Spicy Bean Tamales.

- Double the Texas-Style Barbecue Sauce recipe when making the Jackfruit Barbecue Sandwiches to use for the Baked Barbecue Cauliflower Wings in Week 2.
- Double the Spanish Chorizo recipe when making Tex-Mex Taco Salad to use in the Spanish Chorizo and Vegetable Paella.

WEEK 2

CHECK BEFORE YOU SHOP

Agave nectar
All-purpose flour
Canola oil
Ketchup
Liquid smoke
Maple syrup
Mustard, yellow
Nutritional yeast
Olive oil
Olive oil spray
Soy sauce
Sugar, confectioners'
Sugar, dark brown
Tamari
Toasted sesame oil
Vegetable oil
Vegetable oil spray
Vinegar, apple cider
Vinegar, balsamic
Vinegar, red wine
Worcestershire sauce, vegan

PANTRY SHOPPING LIST

Artichoke hearts, canned (4 hearts)
Barbecue sauce (small jar)
Basil pesto, jarred (¼ cup)
Beans, black, canned (one 15-ounce cans)
Beans, red, canned (three 15-ounce cans)
Bread: burger buns, vegan (4)
Bread: English muffins (6)
Bread: hoagie rolls, vegan (4)
Bread: naan, vegan (4)
Cashews, raw, unsalted (3 cups)
Chia seeds (2 tablespoons)
Chickpeas, canned (15 ounces)
Coconut flakes, unsweetened (½ cup)
Coconut milk, unsweetened, full-fat, canned (2 cups)
Curry powder, Jamaican or regular (1½ teaspoons)

Dill pickle, jarred (8 slices)
Flax meal (3 tablespoons)
Lentils, cooked, canned (2 cups)
Marinara sauce (¼ cup)
Panko bread crumbs, vegan (2 cups)
Pine nuts (¼ cup)
Pumpkin seeds (¼ cup)
Red salsa (1 small jar)
Rice, arborio or short-grain white (2 cups)
Rice, long-grain white (2 cups)
Rigatoni, dried (1 pound)
Rolled oats, old-fashioned (4 cups)
Saffron threads (1 teaspoon)
Semisweet chocolate chips, vegan (1 cup)
Tomato sauce, canned (15 ounces)
Tostadas, in box (8)
Vegetable broth (5 cups)
Walnut pieces (½ cup)

PRODUCE AND PERISHABLES SHOPPING LIST

American-style cheese, vegan (4 slices)
Avocado, Hass (5)
Baby spinach (1 cup)
Bananas, ripe (2 medium)
Bell pepper, green (1 small)
Bell pepper, red (2 medium)
Blueberries (1 cup)
Carrot (1 medium)
Cauliflower (1 head)
Celery (1 stalk)
Cheddar cheese, vegan (½ cup shredded)
Coconut yogurt, plain (2 cups)
Corn, sweet (1 ear)
Cucumber, English (1 large)
Garlic (8 cloves, or 1 head)
Herbs, fresh: chives, cilantro, mint, parsley (small bunch each); rosemary sprig
Italian sausage, plant-based (2 links)
Jalapeño pepper (1 medium)
Lemon (1)
Limes (7)
Mangos (2 large or 4 small)
Oat milk, unsweetened (1 cup)
Onions, yellow (3 medium)
Oyster mushrooms (12 ounces)
Parmesan cheese, vegan (2 tablespoons grated)
Peas, frozen (½ cup)
Plantains, ripe (2 large)
Portobello mushrooms (4 large)

Potatoes, russet (4 large)
Shallots (2 medium)
Soymilk, unsweetened (2 cups)
Tempeh (four 8-ounce packages)
Tofu, extra-firm (2 pounds)
Tofurky kielbasa (2 links)
Tomatoes, Roma (plum) (2 large)
Vegan butter (6 tablespoons)
Watermelon, seedless (1 small)

PREP TIPS

- For the Balsamic Reduction in the Watermelon, Cucumber, and Mint Salad, use leftovers from the Crostini with Macadamia Ricotta, Strawberries, and Basil in Week 1.
- When making the Pan-Sautéed Sweet Plantains, double the recipe to use for the Caribbean Jerk Tempeh Bowls later in the week.
- Save leftover Cashew Cream from Week 1 for the Caribbean Jerk Tempeh Bowls and Loaded English Jacket Potatoes.
- When making Tempeh Bacon for the Loaded English Jacket Potatoes, double the recipe to use for Tofu Eggs Benedict on Sunday.
- Use leftover Cashew Hollandaise from Tofu Eggs Benedict in Week 1 for Tofu Eggs Benedict in week 2.

WEEK 3

CHECK BEFORE YOU SHOP

Agave nectar
Liquid smoke
Maple syrup
Mustard, Dijon
Nutritional yeast
Olive oil
Peanut butter, unsweetened, creamy
Soy sauce
Tamari
Toasted sesame oil
Vegan mayonnaise
Vegetable oil
Vegetable oil spray
Vinegar, apple cider
Vinegar, red wine
Worcestershire sauce, vegan

PANTRY SHOPPING LIST

Beans, black, canned (2 cups)
Bread: English muffins (2)
Bread: French baguettes, vegan (4)
Bread: hoagie rolls, vegan (4)
Capers (1 teaspoon)
Cashews, raw, unsalted (3 cups)
Chia seeds (1 tablespoon)
Chickpeas, canned (two 15-ounce cans)
Chipotle sauce, bottled (2 tablespoons)
Cocoa powder, unsweetened (¼ cup)
Coconut milk, unsweetened, full-fat, canned (2 cups)
Corn, canned, yellow or white (1¼ cups)
Corn tortillas (20)
Cranberries, dried (¼ cup)
Dill pickle, jarred (16 slices)
Dill pickle relish, jarred (1 tablespoon)
Dulse seaweed flakes (1 teaspoon)
Flax meal (3 tablespoons)
Lentils, French green (1 cup)
Louisiana hot sauce, bottled (1 tablespoon)
Panko bread crumbs, vegan (2 cups)
Pine nuts (½ cup)
Pumpkin seeds (¾ cup)
Quinoa (2½ cups)
Rice, brown (1 cup)
Sriracha hot sauce, bottled (1 teaspoon)
Tomato paste, canned (1 tablespoon)
Tomato sauce, canned (1 tablespoon)
Tomatoes, crushed, canned (28 ounces)
Tomatoes, diced, canned (15 ounces)
Vegetable broth (6 cups)
Vinegar, rice wine (1 tablespoon)
Vinegar, sherry (3 tablespoons)

PRODUCE AND PERISHABLES SHOPPING LIST

Avocado, Hass (3)
Baby greens, mixed (4 cups)
Baby kale (4 ounces)
Baby spinach (1 cup)
Bananas, ripe (4 medium)
Brussels sprouts (8 ounces)
Carrots (3 large)
Cauliflower (1 head)
Celery (2 stalks)
Cheese of choice, vegan (½ cup shredded)
Comice pear (1)
Corn kernels, frozen (1 cup)
Cremini mushrooms (2 cups)
Cucumber, English (1 large)
Edamame, fresh, shelled (1 cup)

French fries, frozen (1 package)
Garlic (10 cloves, or 1 head)
Ginger, fresh (2 tablespoons minced)
Guacamole, jarred (½ cup)
Herbs, fresh: basil, dill, lavender, rosemary, chives (small bunch each); cilantro (2 bunches)
Iceberg lettuce (3 cups torn)
Jalapeño pepper (2 small)
Lemon (1 small)
Limes (11)
Oat milk, unsweetened (2 cups)
Onions, yellow (4 medium)
Oyster mushrooms (24 ounces)
Peas, frozen (⅓ cup)
Pineapple, fresh, in rings (4)
Portobello mushrooms (8 large)
Potatoes, Yukon Gold (1½ pounds)
Radicchio (1 head)
Radishes (2)
Red salsa, fresh (½ cup)
Scallions (4)
Shallot (1 small)
Tempeh (8-ounce package)
Tofu, extra-firm (1-pound package)
Tofu, firm (1-pound package)
Tofurky kielbasa (2 links)
Tomato, ripe, any type (¼ diced)
Tomatoes, Roma (plum) (6)
Vegan butter (¾ cup)

PREP TIPS

- When making the Aquafaba Mayo for the Crispy Cauliflower Po' Boys, save leftovers for the Portobello-Pineapple Poke Bowls and Seared Oyster Mushroom Tortas later in the week.
- Use leftover Easy Guacamole and Salsa Fresca from the Seared Oyster Mushroom Tortas for the Southwestern Black Bean and Quinoa Bowls.
- Use leftover Cashew Cream from the Seitan Chorizo Tacos for the Southwestern Black Bean and Quinoa Bowls.
- Use leftover Chunky Red Salsa from Tex-Mex Migas for the Seitan Chorizo Tacos.

WEEK 4

CHECK BEFORE YOU SHOP

Agave nectar
Liquid smoke
Maple syrup
Mustard, Dijon
Mustard, dry (powdered)
Nutritional yeast
Olive oil
Soy sauce
Sugar, granulated
Tamari
Tapioca starch
Toasted sesame oil
Truffle oil
Vegan mayonnaise
Vegetable oil
Vegetable oil spray
Vinegar, apple cider
Vinegar, red wine
Wine, dry white
Worcestershire sauce, vegan

PANTRY SHOPPING LIST

Almonds, raw, unsalted (½ cup)
Beans, black, canned (15 ounces)
Beans, pinto, canned (15 ounces)
Beans, red kidney, canned (2 15-ounce cans)
Beans, white, canned (⅓ cup)
Bread: burger buns, vegan (4)
Bread: English muffins (2)
Bread: French baguette (4 slices)
Bread: hoagie rolls, vegan (4)
Bread: loaf of choice, vegan (8 slices)
Capers (2 tablespoons)
Cashews, raw, unsalted (4 cups)
Chia seeds (¼ cup)
Chickpeas, canned (four 15-ounce cans)
Coconut cream, unsweetened, canned (8 ounces)
Coconut flakes, unsweetened (1 cup)
Coconut milk, unsweetened, canned (2 cups)
Corn, canned (¼ cup)
Corn tortillas (20)
Dates, pitted (2 or 3)
Elbow pasta, dried (1 pound)
Hemp seeds (2 tablespoons)
Macadamia nuts, raw, unsalted (1 cup)
Pumpkin seeds (¼ cup)
Quick oats (½ cup)
Quinoa, tricolored (1½ cups)
Red salsa, jarred (½ cup)
Rice, long-grain white (2 cups)
Rice, short-grain brown (2½ cups)
Rolled oats, old-fashioned (6 cups)

Sweet potato puree, canned (½ cup)
Tomato paste, canned (3 tablespoons)
Tomatoes, crushed, canned (two 28-ounce cans)
Tomatoes, sun-dried, packed in oil (2 tablespoons)
Vegetable broth (12 cups)
Vital wheat gluten (1 cup)
Walnut pieces (½ cup)

PRODUCE AND PERISHABLES SHOPPING LIST

Almond milk, unsweetened
Avocados, Hass (4)
Baby arugula (5 ounces)
Baby spinach (2 cups)
Bananas, ripe (4 medium)
Beets, golden (2 medium)
Beets, red (2 medium)
Bell pepper, green (1 medium)
Bell pepper, red (3 medium)
Blackberries (1½ cups)
Blueberries (2½ cups)
Butternut squash (1 small)
Carrot (1 medium)
Celery (3 stalks)
Cheddar cheese, vegan (1 cup shredded)
Coconut yogurt, plain (2 cups)
Cream cheese, vegan (8 ounces)
Edamame, shelled, frozen (¼ cup)
Garlic cloves (8 to 10 cloves, or 1 head)
Ginger, fresh (1 tablespoon minced)
Guacamole, jarred (½ cup)
Herbs, fresh: basil, dill, cilantro, chives, parsley (small bunch each)
Iceberg lettuce (8 leaves)
Jalapeño pepper (2 medium)
Lemon (1)
Limes (9)
Mangos (2 large or 4 small)
Mozzarella cheese, vegan (½ cup shredded)
Oat milk, unsweetened (2½ cups)
Onion, red (3 small)
Onions, yellow (7 small)
Parmesan cheese, vegan (¼ cup grated)
Pineapple, fresh (1 cup diced)
Plantain, ripe (1 medium)
Portobello mushrooms (4 large)
Provolone cheese, vegan (4 slices)
Raspberries (½ cup)
Romaine lettuce (2 heads)
Scallions (1 bunch of 6)
Shallot (1 small)
Strawberries (½ cup)
Tempeh (three 8-ounce packages)

Tofu, extra-firm (1 pound)
Tomato, ripe, any variety (¼ diced)
Tomatoes, beefsteak or heirloom (3 medium)
Vegan butter (8 ounces)
Wild mushrooms of choice (1½ pounds)

PREP TIPS

- Use leftover Cashew Cream from week 3 for the Easy Three-Bean Chili and Seared Portobello Fajitas.
- Double the recipe for the Italian-Herbed Roasted Chickpeas for the Caesar Salad.
- Use leftover Aquafaba Mayo from the Classic Chick-Free Salad for the Tempeh BLTs and Caribbean Island Burger with Mango Relish.
- Use the Restaurant-Style Chunky Red Salsa leftover from the Tex-Mex Migas for the Seared Portobello Fajitas.
- Cook a double batch of Tempeh Bacon from the Tempeh BLTs for Caesar Salad and Tofu Eggs Benedict.
- Use leftover Cashew Hollandaise from Tofu Eggs Benedict in Week 3 for Tofu Eggs Benedict in Week 4.

Part II

The Recipes

Berry Superfood Smoothie Bowls, page 59

CHAPTER FOUR

Breakfast

Tofu Eggs 3 Ways
- Scrambled Tofu Eggs 54
- Fried Tofu Eggs 55
- Tex-Mex Tofu Scramble 55

Quinoa-Amaranth Porridge with Dried Cranberries and Pumpkin Seeds 57

Berry Superfood Smoothie Bowls 58

Blueberry Oatmeal with Walnuts, Banana, and Coconut 59

Easy Overnight Oats 60

Tex-Mex Migas 61

Tofu Eggs Benedict with Tempeh Bacon, Wilted Spinach, and Cashew Hollandaise 62

Avocado Toast-adas 63

Portobello Steak and Tofu Eggs with Oven Home Fries 64

Tofu Egg Sandwiches 65

Tofu Eggs 3 Ways

Tofu, essential in any vegan kitchen, is an excellent source of protein, iron, and calcium. I love it for its incredible versatility. For this multi-recipe breakfast special, we'll use tofu to make breakfast eggs three ways. Scrambled tofu eggs are perfect with buttery toast for a quick morning pick-me-up. We'll also use them in Portobello Steak and Tofu Eggs with Oven Home Fries (page 64). Fried tofu eggs are the heart of Tofu Eggs Benedict with Tempeh Bacon, Wilted Spinach, and Cashew Hollandaise (page 62). You can also use these delightfully golden patties to give any sandwich a protein punch. Closing out our tofu trio is my Tex-Mex Tofu Scramble, which is an ode to my South Texas roots. Yeehaw! Or perhaps ¡Olé!

Scrambled Tofu Eggs

SERVES 4

PREP TIME: 10 minutes

COOK TIME: 15 minutes

30 MINUTES OR LESS, GLUTEN-FREE, NUT-FREE, ONE POT

- **1 teaspoon vegetable oil**
- **½ teaspoon ground turmeric**
- **1 pound firm tofu, drained, broken into chunks (see Pro Tip, page 56)**
- **½ teaspoon onion powder**
- **½ teaspoon garlic powder**
- **¼ teaspoon ground cumin**
- **½ teaspoon salt**
- **¼ teaspoon black pepper**
- **⅛ teaspoon black Himalayan salt (optional)**

1. In a large skillet over medium-high heat, heat the oil.
2. Add the turmeric and toast for 1 minute, stirring occasionally.
3. Add the tofu and mash with a potato masher.
4. Stir in the onion powder, garlic powder, cumin, salt, pepper, and Himalayan salt (if using). Cook for 5 to 10 minutes, stirring occasionally. Serve.

Per serving: Calories: 99; Total Fat: 6g; Saturated Fat: 1g; Trans Fat: 0g; Total Carbs: 2g; Fiber: 1g; Protein: 9g; Sodium: 450mg; Sugars: 1g

Fried Tofu Eggs

GLUTEN-FREE, NUT-FREE

SERVES 4

PREP TIME: 10 minutes, plus 15 minutes to marinate

COOK TIME: 10 minutes

2 tablespoons vegetable oil
1 teaspoon ground turmeric
1 teaspoon onion powder
1 teaspoon garlic powder
½ teaspoon ground cumin
½ teaspoon salt
½ teaspoon black Himalayan salt (optional)
½ teaspoon black pepper
1 pound extra-firm tofu, drained, cut into ¼-inch cutlets (see Pro Tip, page 62)
Vegetable oil spray

1. In a small bowl, whisk the oil, turmeric, onion powder, garlic powder, cumin, salt, Himalayan salt (if using), and pepper.
2. Place the tofu cutlets on a large plate and generously coat both sides with the marinade. Let marinate for 10 to 15 minutes.
3. Heat a large nonstick skillet or griddle to medium heat.
4. Generously coat the skillet with oil spray and sear the marinated cutlets for 5 minutes on each side.

Per serving: Calories: 168; Total Fat: 14g; Saturated Fat: 1g; Trans Fat: 0g; Total Carbs: 2g; Fiber: 1g; Protein: 11g; Sodium: 300mg; Sugars: 1g

Tex-Mex Tofu Scramble

30 MINUTES OR LESS, GLUTEN-FREE, NUT-FREE, ONE POT

SERVES 4

PREP TIME: 15 minutes

COOK TIME: 15 minutes

2 teaspoons vegetable oil
¼ cup diced yellow onion
¼ teaspoon salt
1 garlic clove, minced
¼ cup diced ripe tomato
¼ cup canned yellow or white corn
½ jalapeño pepper, seeded and finely diced
1 recipe Scrambled Tofu Eggs (page 54)
1 cup firmly packed fresh baby spinach

1. In a large skillet over medium heat, heat the oil.
2. Add the onion and salt. Sauté for 3 to 5 minutes, stirring occasionally.
3. Stir in the garlic. Sauté for 1 minute, stirring occasionally.

CONTINUED

Tofu Eggs 3 Ways CONTINUED

4. Add the tomato, corn, jalapeño, and scrambled tofu eggs and stir to combine. Cook for 3 to 5 minutes, stirring occasionally.
5. Fold in the spinach and toss together until the spinach is wilted. Serve.

Pro Tip: *Extra-firm silken tofu, which is a shelf-stable tofu typically found in the ethnic foods section of your local grocer, is a yummy choice for Scrambled Tofu Eggs (page 54). For Fried Tofu Eggs (page 55), it's vital to use cotton tofu, the kind you find in the refrigerated cases.*

Per serving: Calories: 166; Total Fat: 9g; Saturated Fat: 1g; Trans Fat: 0g; Total Carbs: 12g; Fiber: 2g; Protein: 11g; Sodium: 608mg; Sugars: 2g

Quinoa-Amaranth Porridge with Dried Cranberries and Pumpkin Seeds

SERVES 4

PREP TIME: 5 minutes

COOK TIME: 25 minutes

Quinoa and amaranth, sister superfoods, have been cultivated in Latin America since ancient times. Both are packed with protein, fiber, amino acids, and a host of micronutrients, such as manganese, magnesium, and phosphorus. What makes quinoa and amaranth special in the world of grains is that neither is actually a grain. They are seeds, often referred to as "pseudo-cereals" (neither cereals nor grains), but they share comparable qualities and nutrients.

30 MINUTES OR LESS, GLUTEN-FREE, NUT-FREE, OIL-FREE, ONE POT, SOY-FREE

1½ cups water
¼ teaspoon salt
½ cup quinoa
½ cup amaranth
2 cups unsweetened oat milk
1 tablespoon chia seeds
3 tablespoons agave nectar, divided
¼ cup dried cranberries
¼ cup pumpkin seeds

1. In a medium saucepan, bring the water and salt to a boil.
2. Add the quinoa and amaranth. Reduce the heat to a simmer. Cover the pan and cook for 15 minutes, or until all the liquid is absorbed.
3. Add the oat milk, chia seeds, and 1 tablespoon of the agave. Increase the heat to medium and cook for 5 minutes, stirring constantly, until the porridge is creamy.
4. Serve in small bowls topped with the remaining 2 tablespoons of agave and the cranberries and pumpkin seeds.

Pro Tip: *I love pairing chia seeds with quinoa and amaranth because of their similar Latin American origins. If you don't have chia seeds, use ground flaxseed. The most important thing is to add a punch of omega-3s to this nutty, nutritious breakfast.*

Per serving: Calories: 329; Total Fat: 9g; Saturated Fat: 1g; Trans Fat: 0g; Total Carbs: 53g; Fiber: 5g; Protein: 9g; Sodium: 258mg; Sugars: 14g

SERVES 4

PREP TIME:
20 minutes

Berry Superfood Smoothie Bowls

A few years ago, while vacationing in Tulum, Mexico—a magical place on the Mayan Riviera with historic ruins, crystal-clear beaches, and unimaginable jungle architecture—I met friends at a restaurant for breakfast and found a lot of smoothie bowls on the menu. I didn't get it; I ordered one anyway. When it arrived, I totally got it. It was so thick and rich and beautifully decorated that it had to be eaten with a spoon. I'm now a big fan, and this one takes me back to that breathtaking vacation.

30 MINUTES OR LESS, GLUTEN-FREE, OIL-FREE, ONE POT, SOY-FREE

½ cup fresh strawberries, quartered
½ cup fresh raspberries
½ cup fresh blackberries
1½ cups fresh blueberries, divided
2 ripe bananas, frozen
¾ cup old-fashioned rolled oats
½ small ripe Hass avocado, cubed
2 tablespoons hemp seeds
2 or 3 pitted dates
1½ cups unsweetened oat milk, plus more as needed
Pinch salt
¼ cup pumpkin seeds
¼ cup unsweetened coconut flakes
2 tablespoons chia seeds

1. In a large blender, combine the strawberries, raspberries, blackberries, ½ cup of the blueberries, bananas, oats, avocado, hemp seeds, dates, oat milk, and salt. Blend on high speed until smooth.
2. Serve immediately in small, deep bowls, garnished with the pumpkin seeds, coconut, chia seeds, and the remaining 1 cup of blueberries.

Pro Tip: *Swap fresh berries for frozen mixed berries. Thaw the berries for 10 to 15 minutes before blending.*

Per serving: Calories: 395; Total Fat: 16g; Saturated Fat: 5g; Trans Fat: 0g; Total Carbs: 58g; Fiber: 14g; Protein: 10g; Sodium: 143mg; Sugars: 24g

Blueberry Oatmeal with Walnuts, Banana, and Coconut

SERVES 4

PREP TIME: 5 minutes

COOK TIME: 15 minutes

Oats are one of the healthiest and most nutrient-dense grains on the planet. They are an excellent source of manganese, phosphorous, magnesium, copper, iron, and zinc. They are also rich in antioxidants, including avenanthramides, which can help lower blood pressure. Plus, the soluble fiber in oats can help lower bad LDL cholesterol. This stovetop blueberry oatmeal is simple and satisfying, with a gorgeous purple hue and an extra antioxidant punch from the crushed blueberries.

30 MINUTES OR LESS, GLUTEN-FREE, OIL-FREE, ONE POT, SOY-FREE

3 cups water
1 cup fresh blueberries
2 tablespoons agave nectar
Pinch salt
2 cups old-fashioned rolled oats
1 cup unsweetened oat milk
2 bananas, cut into slices
½ cup walnut pieces, toasted
½ cup unsweetened coconut flakes

1. In a medium saucepan, bring the water and blueberries to a boil. Mash the blueberries with a potato masher. Add the agave, salt, and oats. Reduce the heat to a simmer and cook, uncovered, for about 5 minutes, or until most of the liquid is absorbed.
2. Add the oat milk and simmer for 5 minutes more, until the oatmeal is thick and creamy. Remove from the heat and let cool for 5 minutes.
3. Serve in small, deep bowls topped with the banana, walnuts, and coconut.

Pro Tip: *The trick to getting perfectly creamy oatmeal is to let your oats do their thing. It's tempting to stir and stir the oatmeal as it cooks, but doing so results in a gummy mess.*

Per serving: Calories: 475; Total Fat: 19g; Saturated Fat: 7g; Trans Fat: 0g; Total Carbs: 65g; Fiber: 11g; Protein: 12g; Sodium: 66mg; Sugars: 20g

SERVES 4

PREP TIME:
10 minutes, plus overnight to chill

Easy Overnight Oats

Overnight oats have become a popular food trend everywhere—with everyone Instagramming the latest mason jar creation. An alternative method for preparing oatmeal, overnight oats are simply oats that are soaked overnight to hydrate. This delightful blend can be eaten cold or hot, and is especially good topped with any combination of fruits, seeds, nuts, and spices.

GLUTEN-FREE, OIL-FREE, ONE POT, SOY-FREE

2 cups old-fashioned rolled oats

2 cups plain coconut yogurt

2 tablespoons chia seeds

2 cups canned unsweetened full-fat coconut milk, plus more as needed

2 tablespoons maple syrup

½ teaspoon vanilla extract

1. In a 1-quart mason jar or large sealable glass container, combine the oats, yogurt, chia seeds, coconut milk, maple syrup, and vanilla. Close the lid tightly. Refrigerate overnight.
2. In the morning, add additional coconut milk, if desired. Add garnishes of choice (see headnote).

Pro Tip: *For hot oats, transfer the plumped oats to a medium saucepan and heat over medium heat until warm.*

Per serving: Calories: 370; Total Fat: 13g; Saturated Fat: 7g; Trans Fat: 0g; Total Carbs: 55g; Fiber: 11g; Protein: 9g; Sodium: 15mg; Sugars: 15g

Tex-Mex Migas

SERVES 4

PREP TIME: 10 minutes

COOK TIME: 15 minutes

A staple breakfast in Texas and Tex-Mex spots across the country, migas are a simple mix of day-old pan-toasted corn tortilla wedges scrambled with sautéed onion, tomato, jalapeño, and eggs. The dish originated in Spain, where it's traditionally made with stale bread. This vegan version combines toasted tortilla wedges with a savory and mildly spicy tofu scramble. Top the migas with a generous serving of salsa for a true Tex-Mex experience!

30 MINUTES OR LESS, GLUTEN-FREE, NUT-FREE, ONE POT

2 tablespoons vegetable oil

8 corn tortillas, cut into 1-inch squares

1 recipe Tex-Mex Tofu Scramble (page 55)

½ teaspoon salt, plus more for seasoning

Lime wedges

Avocado slices

Restaurant-Style Chunky Red Salsa (page 136) or store-bought red salsa

1. In a large nonstick pan over medium-high heat, heat the oil. Toast the tortilla squares for about 5 minutes, tossing gently to avoid clumping. When slightly crispy, use a spatula or tongs to transfer the tortillas to a paper towel–lined plate to drain.
2. Place the tofu scramble in the pan and cook for about 5 minutes, stirring occasionally, to warm through.
3. Toss in the tortillas and stir. Season with the salt. Serve hot along with lime wedges, avocado slices, and salsa.

Pro Tip: *For a lower-calorie dish, oven-bake the tortilla wedges for 7 to 10 minutes at 350°F without oil.*

Per serving: Calories: 332; Total Fat: 17g; Saturated Fat: 2g; Trans Fat: 0g; Total Carbs: 33g; Fiber: 5g; Protein: 14g; Sodium: 920mg; Sugars: 2g

SERVES 4

PREP TIME: 15 minutes

COOK TIME: 20 minutes

Tofu Eggs Benedict with Tempeh Bacon, Wilted Spinach, and Cashew Hollandaise

One of my go-to Sunday brunches before going vegan was eggs Benedict. Something about that decadent tower of toasted muffin stacked high with bacon, eggs, and creamy hollandaise brought tears of joy—and sometimes nightmarish heartburn and indigestion. It was one of the first meals I knew I had to give up to get healthy. This vegan version is just as decadent, but with zero risk of salmonella. Black Himalayan salt, also known as kala namak, *is the secret ingredient that provides that yolky flavor we love to tofu eggs and cashew hollandaise.*

ONE POT

1 tablespoon vegan butter or margarine, at room temperature

2 English muffins, split

1 cup loosely packed fresh baby spinach

1 recipe Tempeh Bacon (page 120), warmed

1 recipe Fried Tofu Eggs (page 55), warmed

1 cup Cashew Hollandaise (page 135), warmed

1 teaspoon chopped fresh chives

Dash cayenne pepper (optional)

1. Lightly butter each cut side of the muffins.
2. Heat a large skillet or griddle over medium heat and toast the muffins, cut-side down, for 3 to 4 minutes, or until toasted. Flip the muffins and top each with some of the spinach, tempeh bacon, and a tofu egg.
3. Place 1 muffin half on each plate and generously cover with the hollandaise.
4. Garnish with the chives and cayenne (if using). Serve immediately, with a side of Oven Home Fries (page 118), if desired.

Pro Tip: *When making the tofu eggs for this brunch classic, I cut my tofu cutlets with a round cookie cutter that matches the size of my muffins. It helps make this yummy dish super Instagrammable!*

Per serving: Calories: 612; Total Fat: 43g; Saturated Fat: 8g; Trans Fat: 0g; Total Carbs: 31g; Fiber: 4g; Protein: 31g; Sodium: 1,179mg; Sugars: 4g

Avocado Toast-adas

SERVES 4

PREP TIME: 15 minutes

Why have toast when you can enjoy creamy avocado on a crispy golden tostada? Also called nature's butter, avocados are incredibly nutritious, providing more than a dozen vitamins and minerals, including vitamins C, E, and K, as well as folate and potassium. In fact, avocados outrank bananas in providing potassium, a mineral our bodies need to maintain healthy blood pressure levels.

30 MINUTES OR LESS, GLUTEN-FREE, NUT-FREE, OIL-FREE, SOY-FREE

2 ripe Hass avocados, mashed

1 tablespoon chopped fresh cilantro

Juice of 1 lime

½ teaspoon salt, plus more as needed, divided

1 (15-ounce) can black beans, drained and rinsed

¼ teaspoon garlic powder

¼ teaspoon dark chili powder

8 packaged tostadas

½ cup fresh corn kernels, cut from cob and grilled or roasted

½ cup Salsa Fresca (page 130) or store-bought fresh red salsa

¼ cup pumpkin seeds, toasted

1. In a large bowl, combine the mashed avocado, cilantro, lime juice, and ¼ teaspoon salt (or more to taste).
2. In a medium bowl, toss together the black beans, garlic powder, chili powder, and the remaining ¼ teaspoon of salt (or more to taste). Evenly spread the mashed avocado on each tostada and top with the seasoned beans. Add the corn, salsa, and pumpkin seeds. Serve.

Pro Tip: *Always use ripe avocados when making avocado toast. A ripe avocado is slightly soft to the touch when squeezed gently.*

Per serving: Calories: 433; Total Fat: 14g; Saturated Fat: 2g; Trans Fat: 0g; Total Carbs: 65g; Fiber: 17g; Protein: 13g; Sodium: 947mg; Sugars: 3g

SERVES 4

PREP TIME:
10 minutes, plus 20 minutes to marinate

COOK TIME:
10 minutes

Portobello Steak and Tofu Eggs with Oven Home Fries

Portobello mushrooms star in this healthy spin on the quintessential American diner standard. Portobellos are a great substitute for steak because of their cancer-fighting properties and culinary versatility. For this healthier twist, "steak and eggs" is officially back on the menu—only reimagined!

GLUTEN-FREE, NUT-FREE

2 tablespoons vegetable oil

1 tablespoon tamari

1 tablespoon smoked paprika

1 teaspoon garlic powder

1 teaspoon onion powder

½ teaspoon ground cumin

¼ teaspoon black pepper

4 large portobello mushrooms, stems removed and gills scraped

1 recipe Scrambled Tofu Eggs (page 54), warmed

1 recipe Oven Home Fries (page 118), warmed

1. In a small bowl, whisk together the oil, tamari, paprika, garlic powder, onion powder, cumin, and pepper.
2. Place the mushroom caps on a large plate and evenly coat with the marinade. Let sit for 20 minutes.
3. Preheat a grill to medium-high heat (see Pro Tip). Grill the mushrooms for 4 to 5 minutes per side over direct heat. Serve them hot alongside the warmed scrambled tofu eggs and home fries.

Pro Tip: *If you don't have a grill, fast-sear the mushrooms on the stovetop. Add 1 tablespoon oil to a large cast-iron skillet and heat until hot. Place the mushrooms in the skillet, and use a second smaller skillet or a grill press to press down on the mushrooms. Sear for 3 to 4 minutes per side.*

Per serving: Calories: 345; Total Fat: 20g; Saturated Fat: 3g; Trans Fat: 0g; Total Carbs: 26g; Fiber: 5g; Protein: 14g; Sodium: 1,021mg; Sugars: 5g

Tofu Egg Sandwiches

SERVES 4

PREP TIME: 15 minutes

COOK TIME: 10 minutes

This veganized version of the fast food breakfast staple really hits the spot. With that classic comfort taste and zero cholesterol, now you'll really be lovin' it!

30 MINUTES OR LESS, NUT-FREE, ONE POT

2 tablespoons vegan butter or margarine, melted

4 English muffins, split

4 slices vegan American-style cheese

1 recipe Fried Tofu Eggs (page 55), warmed

1 recipe Tempeh Bacon (page 120), warmed

1. Lightly butter each cut side of the English muffins.
2. Heat a large skillet or griddle over medium heat and toast the muffins, cut-side down, for 3 to 4 minutes, or until toasted. Flip the muffins and top the 4 halves with the cheese, a fried tofu egg, and tempeh bacon. Top with the remaining muffin halves, toasted side down. Continue to toast the sandwiches for 2 minutes per side. Serve hot.

Pro Tip: *My favorite cheese for this recipe is Follow Your Heart's American-style slices—they melt beautifully!*

Per serving: Calories: 412; Total Fat: 25g; Saturated Fat: 6g; Trans Fat: 0g; Total Carbs: 29g; Fiber: 4g; Protein: 17g; Sodium: 1,258mg; Sugars: 3g

Roasted Beet Salad with Baby Arugula and Macadamia Ricotta, page 70

CHAPTER FIVE

Salads

Watermelon, Cucumber, and Mint Salad 68

Frisée and Apple Salad with Walnuts and Pomegranate 69

Roasted Beet Salad with Baby Arugula and Macadamia Ricotta 70

Tropical Quinoa Salad 71

Napa Cabbage Salad 72

Chopped Fall Salad with Herbs 73

Tex-Mex Taco Salad 74

Caesar Salad with Italian-Herbed Roasted Chickpeas 75

Mango Shiitake Ceviche 76

Classic Chick-Free Salad 77

SERVES 4

PREP TIME: 30 minutes

Watermelon, Cucumber, and Mint Salad

This sweet and savory watermelon salad is meant for hot summer days. Every year when July rolls around, I can't get enough of this fruit that provides hydration and essential vitamins, minerals, and antioxidants. Watermelon and cucumber, both members of Cucurbitaceae, combine in this crisp, refreshing treat that is sure to become a summertime favorite.

30 MINUTES OR LESS, GLUTEN-FREE, OIL-FREE, ONE POT, SOY-FREE

1 small (about 1½ pounds) seedless watermelon, peeled and diced (see Pro Tip)

1 large English cucumber, unpeeled, diced

10 fresh mint leaves, chopped

Grated zest of 1 small lemon

Juice of 1 small lemon

¼ teaspoon salt, plus more as needed

¼ cup Balsamic Reduction (page 137)

¼ cup pine nuts, toasted

1. In a large bowl, stir together the watermelon, cucumber, mint, and lemon zest.
2. Add the lemon juice and salt and gently toss. Serve drizzled with the balsamic reduction and sprinkled with the pine nuts.

Pro Tip: *To pick the perfect watermelon, find the field spot, which is where the melon was resting on the ground. It should be firm, with a creamy, buttery color. Knock on the spot—it should sound hollow. A soft or dull-sounding field spot means the melon is beyond its prime.*

Per serving: Calories: 372; Total Fat: 7g; Saturated Fat: 1g; Trans Fat: 0g; Total Carbs: 79g; Fiber: 4g; Protein: 7g; Sodium: 164mg; Sugars: 63g

Frisée and Apple Salad with Walnuts and Pomegranate

SERVES 4

PREP TIME: 15 minutes

Frisée is a variety of endive with curly yellow-green leaves. Its mildly spicy flavor pairs well with bright fruits and dressings. Maple-Cinnamon Vinaigrette strikes the perfect balance here with the frisée, crisp apple, and tangy pomegranate seeds. Toasted walnuts add earthiness and a kick of omega-3s.

30 MINUTES OR LESS, GLUTEN-FREE, ONE POT, SOY-FREE

1 large (6-ounce) head frisée, torn into pieces

1 large Gala apple, cored and thinly sliced

¼ cup Maple-Cinnamon Vinaigrette (page 126)

½ cup pomegranate seeds

¼ cup walnuts, toasted (see Pro Tip)

In a large bowl, combine the frisée and apple. Add the dressing and gently toss. Serve garnished with the pomegranate seeds and walnuts.

Pro Tip: *To toast walnuts, heat a skillet over medium-high heat. Add a single layer of nuts and toast for 5 minutes, stirring frequently. Transfer to a plate to cool.*

Per serving: Calories: 171; Total Fat: 12g; Saturated Fat: 1g; Trans Fat: 0g; Total Carbs: 16g; Fiber: 4g; Protein: 2g; Sodium: 84mg; Sugars: 11g

SERVES 4

PREP TIME:
15 minutes

COOK TIME:
40 minutes

Roasted Beet Salad with Baby Arugula and Macadamia Ricotta

Beets are a nutritional powerhouse and the star of this warm salad. Beets boast an impressive list of health benefits, including their ability to lower blood pressure, improve athletic performance, and support brain health.

GLUTEN-FREE, SOY-FREE

2 red beets, peeled and quartered

2 golden beets, peeled and quartered

1 tablespoon olive oil

1 cup raw unsalted macadamia nuts

1 teaspoon fresh lemon juice

½ teaspoon salt

¼ cup water, plus more as needed

5 ounces baby arugula

¼ cup Red Wine Vinaigrette (page 126) or store-bought vinaigrette

1. Preheat the oven to 350°F.
2. Coat the beets with the oil and place on a baking sheet.
3. Bake for 40 minutes, or until tender.
4. In a food processor, combine the macadamia nuts, lemon juice, salt, and ¼ cup water. Process until smooth, scraping down the sides and adding more water as needed for a smooth mixture.
5. In a large bowl, gently toss the arugula with 2 tablespoons of the vinaigrette. Top each serving of arugula with 2 red beet quarters and 2 yellow beet quarters.
6. Drizzle the remaining 2 tablespoons of dressing over the beets and garnish with a dollop of the macadamia "ricotta."

Pro Tip: *Though this recipe calls for both red and golden beets, use one or the other as you like. Nutritionally, they're similar. Golden beets tend to be sweeter and less earthy in flavor.*

Per serving: Calories: 382; Total Fat: 36g; Saturated Fat: 6g; Trans Fat: 0g; Total Carbs: 16g; Fiber: 6g; Protein: 5g; Sodium: 447mg; Sugars: 9g

Tropical Quinoa Salad

SERVES 4

PREP TIME: 30 minutes, plus chilling

This Miami-inspired tropical quinoa salad is as beautiful and colorful as it is delicious. This nod to my old home features tricolored quinoa and black beans tossed together with fresh pineapple, avocado, cilantro, olive oil, and a squeeze of lime. Toasted coconut flakes add a nice, sweet crunch. This protein-rich salad is perfect for a post-workout snack or a light lunch.

GLUTEN-FREE, ONE POT, SOY-FREE

- 1½ cups tricolored quinoa, cooked according to package directions, chilled
- 1 cup canned black beans, drained, rinsed, and chilled
- 1 cup diced fresh pineapple
- ½ small red onion, finely diced
- ½ red bell pepper, finely diced
- 2 tablespoons chopped fresh cilantro
- 1 tablespoon olive oil
- Juice of 1 lime
- 1 teaspoon salt, plus more as needed
- ¼ teaspoon black pepper
- 1 Hass avocado, diced
- ¼ cup unsweetened coconut flakes, toasted

1. In a large bowl, stir together the quinoa, black beans, pineapple, red onion, bell pepper, cilantro, olive oil, lime juice, salt, and pepper.
2. Add the avocado and gently toss. Top with the toasted coconut and serve.

Pro Tip: *Swap the pineapple for any other tropical fruit to add variety. I love this salad with mango, papaya, or dragon fruit.*

Per serving: Calories: 284; Total Fat: 13g; Saturated Fat: 4g; Trans Fat: 0g; Total Carbs: 37g; Fiber: 11g; Protein: 8g; Sodium: 822mg; Sugars: 7g

SERVES 4

PREP TIME: 20 minutes

Napa Cabbage Salad

Napa cabbage comes to life with a sweet and savory peanut sauce for this Thai-inspired salad. Napa cabbage is loaded with antioxidants, which can help fight free radicals in the body. It's also high in vitamin C, which helps the body battle infection.

30 MINUTES OR LESS, GLUTEN-FREE, ONE POT

1 small head napa cabbage, cored and shredded (see Pro Tip)

1 medium English cucumber, cored and julienned

1 small red bell pepper, julienned

1 medium carrot, grated

2 scallions, green parts only, sliced

¼ cup fresh cilantro, chopped, divided

½ cup Peanut Sauce (page 131)

½ cup peanuts, roasted and chopped

1. In a large bowl, combine the cabbage, cucumber, bell pepper, carrot, scallion greens, and 2 tablespoons of the cilantro. Add the peanut sauce and toss to coat.
2. Serve garnished with the roasted peanuts and the remaining 2 tablespoons of cilantro.

Pro Tip: *Any type of cabbage works well for this recipe. I like napa cabbage because it's milder in flavor and more tender than most cabbage varieties.*

Per serving: Calories: 308; Total Fat: 18g; Saturated Fat: 3g; Trans Fat: 0g; Total Carbs: 29g; Fiber: 9g; Protein: 13g; Sodium: 462mg; Sugars: 10g

Chopped Fall Salad with Herbs

SERVES 4

PREP TIME: 20 minutes

Antioxidant-rich radicchio, Brussels sprouts, kale, and aromatic herbs are the base of this chopped salad, drizzled with a delicate vinaigrette and topped with a red Comice pear and toasted pine nuts for a sophisticated bowl of reds and greens. It's the perfect accompaniment for the Tofu Chops with Caramelized Apple and Onion (page 151).

30 MINUTES OR LESS, GLUTEN-FREE, ONE POT, SOY-FREE

- **1 (8-ounce) head radicchio, chopped (see Pro Tip)**
- **8 ounces Brussels sprouts, trimmed and thinly sliced**
- **4 ounces baby kale**
- **½ cup assorted fresh herbs (basil, dill, lavender, rosemary), finely chopped**
- **1 ripe red Comice pear, cored and cubed**
- **¼ cup Red Wine Vinaigrette (page 126) or store-bought vinaigrette**
- **½ cup pine nuts, toasted**

1. In a large bowl, combine the radicchio, Brussels sprouts, kale, herbs, and pear.
2. Add the vinaigrette and gently toss to coat. Serve immediately, garnished with the pine nuts.

Pro Tip: *Radicchio is what gives this salad its complex, mildly bitter notes. Can't find radicchio? Swap it for any other peppery green, such as arugula, endive, or mustard greens.*

Per serving: Calories: 220; Total Fat: 16g; Saturated Fat: 3g; Trans Fat: 0g; Total Carbs: 18g; Fiber: 6g; Protein: 4g; Sodium: 101mg; Sugars: 8g

SERVES 4

PREP TIME: 10 minutes

COOK TIME: 15 minutes

Tex-Mex Taco Salad

Taco salad gets a vegan makeover in this reimagined Tex-Mex classic. Crisp romaine lettuce is topped with corn chips and seitan chorizo crumbles sautéed with a blend of spicy seasonings to bring that Texas heat. We finish the taco salad with shredded vegan cheese, cherry tomatoes, avocado wedges, diced onion, tangy Cashew Cream, and a smoky Agave-Chipotle Vinaigrette. This salad travels well, so make it for your next Taco Tuesday picnic or potluck to impress your friends.

30 MINUTES OR LESS, ONE POT

- 1 teaspoon vegetable oil
- 1 recipe Spanish Chorizo (page 106) or 4 links Tofurky kielbasa, chopped or crumbled
- 1½ teaspoons dark chili powder
- 1 teaspoon chipotle powder
- ½ teaspoon garlic powder
- ½ teaspoon dried oregano
- 1 tablespoon tomato sauce
- 1 large head romaine lettuce, chopped
- 4 ounces corn chips
- ½ cup shredded vegan cheddar or pepper Jack cheese
- 1 cup cherry tomatoes, sliced into halves
- 1 Hass avocado, sliced into wedges
- ¼ small red onion, finely diced
- ¼ cup Cashew Cream (page 139)
- ¼ cup Agave-Chipotle Vinaigrette (page 127) or store-bought spicy vinaigrette

1. In a skillet over medium-high heat, heat the oil. Add the chorizo, chili powder, chipotle powder, garlic powder, oregano, and tomato sauce and toss together. Sauté for 5 to 7 minutes, until nicely browned.

2. Layer the lettuce on individual plates. Top each with some corn chips, the chorizo mixture, the cheese, tomatoes, avocado, and red onion. Drizzle with the cashew cream and serve the vinaigrette alongside.

Pro Tip: *For a gluten-free salad, swap the chorizo for 3 cups canned black beans, drained and rinsed. Sauté for 5 to 7 minutes with 1 tablespoon vegetable oil and the seasonings listed, plus ½ teaspoon salt and some pepper to taste.*

Per serving: Calories: 678; Total Fat: 34g; Saturated Fat: 4g; Trans Fat: 0g; Total Carbs: 46g; Fiber: 10g; Protein: 51g; Sodium: 1,149mg; Sugars: 7g

Caesar Salad with Italian-Herbed Roasted Chickpeas

SERVES 4

PREP TIME: 45 minutes

This guilt-free twist on the classic Caesar salad is going to have friends and fam begging for more. Cashews and capers form the base for our fish-free and egg-free dressing. And Italian-herbed chickpeas step in for the croutons, supplying added protein. This rich, hearty salad is perfect on its own or accompanied by any sandwich or entrée for a more robust meal.

GLUTEN-FREE, ONE POT

- **1 large head romaine lettuce, chopped**
- **½ cup Cashew Caesar Dressing (page 128) or store-bought vegan Caesar dressing**
- **1 recipe Italian-Herbed Roasted Chickpeas (page 114)**
- **½ cup Tempeh Bacon (optional; page 120)**
- **2 tablespoons grated vegan Parmesan cheese**

In a large bowl, toss together the lettuce and dressing. Serve immediately, garnished with the chickpeas, tempeh bacon (if using), and Parmesan.

Pro Tip: *Although the tempeh bacon is optional, do yourself—and your loved ones—a favor and take the time to make it. It elevates this salad to the next level.*

Per serving: Calories: 181; Total Fat: 8g; Saturated Fat: 1g; Trans Fat: 0g; Total Carbs: 21g; Fiber: 6g; Protein: 8g; Sodium: 589mg; Sugars: 4g

SERVES 4

PREP TIME:
20 minutes, plus
1 hour to chill

Mango Shiitake Ceviche

Typically made with raw fish or seafood cured in lime juice, ceviche is a popular dish loved around the world for its refreshing flavors and unique textures. This vegan spin on the Peruvian mainstay features elegant shiitake mushrooms, which do a wonderful job mimicking the texture of shellfish. Red bell pepper and onion add a nice crunch and mango rounds out our ceviche on a sweet note.

GLUTEN-FREE, NUT-FREE, ONE POT, SOY-FREE

1 large mango, peeled and diced
1 cup shiitake mushrooms, stems removed and caps julienned
½ red bell pepper, finely diced
¼ small red onion, finely diced
¼ cup fresh cilantro, finely chopped
½ teaspoon salt
¼ teaspoon black pepper
1 Hass avocado, diced
Juice of 2 limes
1 tablespoon olive oil

1. In a large bowl, combine the mango, mushrooms, bell pepper, onion, cilantro, salt, and pepper.
2. Add the avocado, lime juice, and olive oil and gently toss to combine. Chill for about 1 hour.
3. Serve on its own or with crackers or corn chips, if desired.

Pro Tip: *For added seafood flavor, toss in ½ teaspoon kelp or dulse seaweed flakes.*

Per serving: Calories: 182; Total Fat: 9g; Saturated Fat: 1g; Trans Fat: 0g; Total Carbs: 25g; Fiber: 6g; Protein: 3g; Sodium: 299mg; Sugars: 17g

Classic Chick-Free Salad

SERVES 4

PREP TIME:
20 minutes, plus
1 hour to chill

Chickpeas—or garbanzo beans—star in this plant-based twist on classic chicken salad. Their versatility and lightly nutty taste make them a perfect plant protein to combine with a variety of flavors and textures. This version is extra special because it uses aquafaba—chickpea water—to make a citrusy and delightfully creamy mayonnaise. Tossed together with the traditional combination of celery, scallions, and fresh dill, this chick-free salad is sure to become one of your new favorites.

GLUTEN-FREE, NUT-FREE, ONE POT, SOY-FREE

2 (15-ounce) cans chickpeas, strained (reserve liquid for another use) and rinsed

2 celery stalks, diced

2 scallions, green parts only, diced

2 teaspoons finely chopped fresh dill

⅓ cup Aquafaba Mayo (page 141) or store-bought vegan mayo

1 to 2 teaspoons Dijon mustard

¼ teaspoon salt, plus more as needed

Pinch black pepper

Romaine lettuce leaves

1. Place the chickpeas in a medium bowl and lightly mash with a fork or potato masher, leaving some whole.
2. Add the celery, scallions, and dill. Use a spoon or spatula to fold together.
3. Add the mayo, mustard, salt, and pepper. Mix well. Cover and chill for about 1 hour.
4. Serve atop lettuce leaves and with crackers, if desired.

Pro Tip: *For a seafood salad, add 1 tablespoon dulse flakes or any other chopped or pulverized seaweed. Nori, the seaweed typically used for sushi, can be pulverized easily in a dry, clean blender or coffee grinder.*

Per serving: Calories: 403; Total Fat: 18g; Saturated Fat: 1g; Trans Fat: 0g; Total Carbs: 50g; Fiber: 10g; Protein: 11g; Sodium: 940mg; Sugars: 1g

Tex-Mex Tortilla Soup, page 85

CHAPTER SIX

Soups and Stews

French Onion Soup 80

Mom's Homestyle Lentil Soup 81

Cream of Broccoli Soup 82

Watermelon-Mint Gazpacho 83

Thick and Hearty Minestrone 84

Tex-Mex Tortilla Soup 85

Easy Three-Bean Chili 86

Roasted Butternut Squash Soup 87

Quick Cuban Black Bean Soup 88

Hearty Vegetable Stew 89

SERVES 4

PREP TIME:
25 minutes

COOK TIME:
1 hour 10 minutes

French Onion Soup

Instead of the typical beef broth, our French onion soup calls for vegetable broth seasoned with soy sauce, vegan Worcestershire, and liquid smoke to bring that beefiness. Like the traditional version, we caramelize the onions before simmering them in a moo-free broth, then top the soup with toasted French bread oozing with vegan provolone. Bon appétit!

⅓ cup vegan butter or margarine
2 tablespoons olive oil, divided
4 small yellow onions, julienned
½ teaspoon sugar
1 garlic clove, minced
½ cup dry white wine
6 cups vegetable broth
2 tablespoons soy sauce
1 teaspoon vegan Worcestershire sauce or steak sauce
1 teaspoon liquid smoke
1 teaspoon dried thyme
Salt and black pepper
4 (1½-inch-thick) French baguette slices, toasted
2 tablespoons grated vegan Parmesan cheese
4 slices vegan provolone cheese

1. In a large soup pot over medium heat, melt the butter. Add 1 tablespoon of the olive oil and the onions. Sauté for 10 to 12 minutes, stirring frequently, until onions are tender and translucent.
2. Add the sugar and continue to cook for 2 to 3 minutes, stirring, until the onions are caramelized. Add the garlic and cook for 1 minute.
3. Deglaze the pot by adding the wine and scraping down the pot.
4. Stir in the broth, soy sauce, Worcestershire sauce, liquid smoke, and thyme. Season with salt and pepper to taste. Increase the heat to bring the soup to a boil, then reduce to a low simmer and cover the pot. Cook for 25 to 30 minutes.
5. Preheat the oven to 450°F. Line a baking sheet with parchment paper.
6. Brush both sides of the bread slices with some of the remaining 1 tablespoon of oil and place on the prepared baking sheet.
7. Toast the bread for 5 to 7 minutes. Remove from the oven and turn the bread slices over. Sprinkle with the Parmesan and top with the provolone. Toast for 2 to 5 minutes, until the cheese melts.
8. Serve the soup topped with the toasts.

Per serving: Calories: 470; Total Fat: 29g; Saturated Fat: 15g; Trans Fat: 0g; Total Carbs: 45g; Fiber: 5g; Protein: 6g; Sodium: 2,108mg; Sugars: 17g

Pro Tip: *Refrigerate the soup in an airtight container for up to 5 days. Freeze in a freezer-safe container for up to 6 months.*

Mom's Homestyle Lentil Soup

SERVES 4

PREP TIME: 20 minutes

COOK TIME: 1 hour

This herbed lentil soup really brings the taste of home. For this one-pot recipe, protein-packed lentils are slow-simmered in a rich, tomatoey broth. This homestyle lentil soup can be served as a meal on its own or as a hearty companion to a light salad or sandwich.

GLUTEN-FREE, NUT-FREE, ONE POT, SOY-FREE

1½ teaspoons vegetable oil

½ medium yellow onion, finely diced

1 large carrot, finely diced

1 celery stalk, finely diced

1 garlic clove, minced

½ teaspoon dried rosemary

½ teaspoon dried thyme

½ teaspoon dried oregano

½ teaspoon dried sage

¼ teaspoon salt, plus more as needed

¼ teaspoon black pepper

2 cups brown or green lentils

1 small russet potato, peeled and finely diced

¼ cup canned crushed tomatoes

6 cups vegetable broth

1. In a large soup pot over medium-high heat, heat the oil. Sauté the onion, carrot, celery, and garlic for 5 minutes.
2. Stir in the rosemary, thyme, oregano, sage, salt, and pepper. Add the lentils, potato, tomatoes, and broth. Bring to a boil. Reduce the heat to a simmer and cover the pot. Cook for 40 to 50 minutes. The lentils should remain firm but be fully cooked. Serve hot.

Did you know? *Lentils are a symbol of good luck and prosperity in many parts of the world. That's why they're so popular around the new year.*

Per serving: Calories: 427; Total Fat: 3g; Saturated Fat: 0g; Trans Fat: 0g; Total Carbs: 73g; Fiber: 33g; Protein: 27g; Sodium: 993mg; Sugars: 6g

SERVES 4

PREP TIME:
10 minutes

COOK TIME:
40 minutes

Cream of Broccoli Soup

Did you know broccoli is a flower? That's why we call bits of its head "florets." Broccoli is a cruciferous vegetable specifically grown for its flower head. Loaded with a wide array of vitamins, minerals, and fiber, this budding beauty gets the spotlight in our creamy, dairy-free version of the classic soup—that's what I call flower power!

GLUTEN-FREE, ONE POT

2 tablespoons vegan butter or margarine
1 small yellow onion, diced
1 celery stalk, diced
¼ teaspoon salt, plus more as needed
3 tablespoons rice flour
4¼ cups vegetable broth
6 cups diced broccoli florets
1½ cups unsweetened soymilk
¼ teaspoon black pepper

1. In a large pot over medium-high heat, melt the butter. Sauté the onion, celery, and salt for 7 to 10 minutes, until tender.
2. Slowly add the flour, stirring constantly to coat the vegetables. Sauté for 1 minute.
3. Little by little, add the broth, stirring to remove any clumps. Bring to a simmer.
4. Add the broccoli and return to a simmer. Cook, uncovered, for 15 to 20 minutes, until the broccoli is tender. Remove from the heat.
5. Using an immersion blender, or transferring to a standard blender in small batches, puree the soup until smooth. Return the soup to the pot if using a standard blender.
6. Stir in the soymilk and heat through. Taste and season with pepper and more salt, if desired.

Pro Tip: *No fresh broccoli? Use frozen. Cook time is the same.*

Per serving: Calories: 194; Total Fat: 8g; Saturated Fat: 4g; Trans Fat: 0g; Total Carbs: 25g; Fiber: 7g; Protein: 8g; Sodium: 798mg; Sugars: 4g

Watermelon-Mint Gazpacho

SERVES 4

PREP TIME:
20 minutes, plus
1 hour to chill

Gazpacho originated in Andalusia, in southern Spain, and the gazpacho we know today consists primarily of tomatoes, which didn't appear in Spain until the 16th century. And this newest iteration features another summer superstar, the watermelon. Blended with ripe summer tomatoes, cucumber, bell pepper, and mint, this sweet and savory cold soup is a wonderful starter for any summer meal!

NUT-FREE, ONE POT, SOY-FREE

FOR THE GAZPACHO

3 ripe Roma (plum) tomatoes, quartered

1 medium cucumber, peeled and roughly chopped

¼ small red bell pepper, roughly chopped

1 medium shallot, peeled and quartered

1 or 2 garlic cloves, quartered

2 cups cubed seedless watermelon

10 to 15 fresh mint leaves

1 tablespoon red wine vinegar

1 teaspoon salt, plus more as needed

Black pepper

1 slice vegan white bread, crust removed, cut into squares

3 to 4 tablespoons extra-virgin olive oil

FOR SERVING (OPTIONAL)

Cucumber, peeled and finely diced

Seedless watermelon, finely diced

Chopped fresh mint leaves

Cashew Cream (page 139)

Vegan bread crumbs

1. **Make the gazpacho:** In a large high-speed blender or food processor, process the tomatoes to a rough puree. Add the cucumber, bell pepper, shallot, garlic, watermelon, mint, vinegar, salt, pepper to taste, and bread. Blend until mostly smooth.
2. With the blender running, slowly pour in the olive oil, blending until the soup is smooth and all ingredients are well integrated. Taste and season with more salt, if needed. Pour the soup into a large container and cover. Chill for at least 1 hour before serving.
3. Serve the chilled soup in bowls and top with garnishes of choice.

Per serving: Calories: 154; Total Fat: 12g; Saturated Fat: 2g; Trans Fat: 0g; Total Carbs: 12g; Fiber: 2g; Protein: 2g; Sodium: 588mg; Sugars: 8g

Origin story: *Did you know the word* gazpacho *comes from the Arabic word for "soaked bread"? In ancient times, ingredients for gazpacho were hand-chopped or crushed with a pestle. Stale bread was added to the mix to moisten it and make it edible again. Modern-day gazpacho is typically made in a blender or food processor, and bread is added as a thickening agent.*

SERVES 4

PREP TIME: 15 minutes

COOK TIME: 30 minutes

Thick and Hearty Minestrone

Rich tomatoey broth is flavored with Italian herbs, fresh veggies, red kidney beans, and pasta for this satisfying homestyle soup. This year-round classic is budget friendly and so easy to make that you'll be cooking it repeatedly. Serve with a side salad for a robust lunch or dinner.

NUT-FREE, ONE POT, SOY-FREE

FOR THE MINESTRONE

2 tablespoons olive oil

½ small yellow onion, diced

1 large carrot, finely diced

1 celery stalk, finely diced

¼ teaspoon salt, plus more as needed

1 medium zucchini, finely diced

2 garlic cloves, minced

½ teaspoon dried rosemary, crushed

½ teaspoon dried parsley

½ teaspoon dried thyme

½ teaspoon dried sage

½ teaspoon dried oregano

¼ teaspoon black pepper

1 (6-ounce) can tomato paste

1 (15-ounce) can diced tomatoes with juice

4 cups vegetable broth

1 (15-ounce) can red kidney beans, drained and rinsed

½ cup short pasta (like elbows or ditalini)

FOR SERVING (OPTIONAL)

Basil Pesto (page 133) or store-bought vegan pesto

Grated vegan Parmesan cheese

Vegan croutons

1. **Make the minestrone:** In a large soup pot over medium-high heat, heat the olive oil. Sauté the onion, carrot, celery, and salt for 7 to 10 minutes, or until the onion is translucent.
2. Stir in the zucchini, garlic, rosemary, parsley, thyme, sage, oregano, pepper, and tomato paste. Sauté for 1 to 2 minutes.
3. Add the tomatoes and their juice and the broth and bring to a boil. Reduce the heat to a simmer and add the kidney beans and pasta. Cook, uncovered, for 8 to 10 minutes, or until pasta is al dente. Taste and season with more salt, if needed.
4. Serve hot, garnished with pesto, Parmesan, and croutons.

Per serving: Calories: 306; Total Fat: 8g; Saturated Fat: 1g; Trans Fat: 0g; Total Carbs: 50g; Fiber: 13g; Protein: 11g; Sodium: 1,562mg; Sugars: 16g

Tex-Mex Tortilla Soup

SERVES 4

PREP TIME: 20 minutes

COOK TIME: 50 minutes

Tortilla soup has a special place in my heart. This easy version of the tortilla soup my Mexican grandma used to make calls for silky oyster mushrooms, which bring a rich umami quality. The trick is to get those mushrooms nicely browned before simmering in a smoky chili broth. To dress a real vegan Tex-Mex tortilla soup, top with pan-fried tortilla strips, vegan cheese shreds, avocado, and a large pinch of fresh cilantro. Oh. So. Good.

NUT-FREE, ONE POT

FOR THE TORTILLA SOUP

1 tablespoon vegetable oil, divided

½ small yellow onion, diced

1 medium carrot, diced

1 celery stalk, diced

2 garlic cloves, minced

2 tablespoons chipotle sauce

1 (15-ounce) can diced tomatoes, with juice

8 ounces fresh oyster mushrooms, separated

1 teaspoon ground cumin

1 teaspoon dried oregano

1 teaspoon black pepper

½ teaspoon salt, plus more as needed

4 cups vegetable broth

1 cup canned corn kernels

2 tablespoons chopped fresh cilantro

Juice of 1 lime

FOR SERVING (OPTIONAL)

4 ounces corn chips or pan-fried tortilla strips

½ cup shredded vegan cheese of choice

1 Hass avocado, cut into wedges

½ cup fresh cilantro, chopped

1. **Make the tortilla soup:** In a large soup pot over medium-high heat, combine 1½ teaspoons of the oil, the onion, carrot, celery, and garlic. Sauté for 7 to 10 minutes, until soft. Transfer to a high-speed blender and add the chipotle sauce and tomatoes with their juice. Blend until smooth.
2. In the same pot over medium-high heat, combine the remaining 1½ teaspoons of oil and the mushrooms. Sauté for 5 to 7 minutes, until nicely browned.
3. Stir in the cumin, oregano, pepper, and salt. Sauté for 1 minute. Pour in the tomato mixture from the blender and simmer for 5 minutes.
4. Add the broth and bring to a boil. Reduce the heat to a simmer and cook, uncovered, for 15 minutes.
5. Add the corn, cilantro, and lime juice. Cook for 5 minutes.
6. Serve hot, topped with corn chips, cheese, avocado, and cilantro, as desired.

Per serving: Calories: 506; Total Fat: 22g; Saturated Fat: 3g; Trans Fat: 0g; Total Carbs: 71g; Fiber: 12g; Protein: 10g; Sodium: 1,395mg; Sugars: 7g

Pro Tip: *I use oyster mushrooms here because they're a perfect swap for the chicken my grandma used in her recipe, but any mushroom works. Use button mushrooms if you're on a budget; try shiitakes for a more complex flavor.*

SERVES 4

PREP TIME: 15 minutes

COOK TIME: 30 minutes

Easy Three-Bean Chili

In some parts of Texas, if you add beans to your chili you can expect an eviction notice. Thankfully, I grew up in a part of Texas where beans are a welcome addition to any dish, even chili. In fact, this version features only *beans! If you think meat is the only way to do chili, you don't know beans!*

GLUTEN-FREE, NUT-FREE, ONE POT

- 1 tablespoon vegetable oil
- 1 small red onion, diced, plus more for serving (optional)
- 1 large jalapeño pepper, seeded and diced, plus slices for serving (optional)
- 3 to 4 garlic cloves, minced
- 1 teaspoon salt, plus more as needed
- 1 tablespoon cumin powder
- 1 teaspoon black pepper, plus more as needed
- 1 (28-ounce) can crushed tomatoes
- 1 (15-ounce) can pinto beans, drained and rinsed
- 1 (15-ounce) can black beans, drained and rinsed
- 1 (15-ounce) can red kidney beans, drained and rinsed
- 2 tablespoons dark chili powder
- 2 teaspoons chipotle powder
- 2 cups vegetable broth
- Juice of 1 lime
- Cashew Cream (page 139)
- Shredded vegan cheddar cheese

1. In a large soup pot over medium heat, heat the oil. Sauté the onion, jalapeño, garlic, and salt for 7 to 10 minutes, until the onion is very tender and almost caramelized.
2. Add the cumin and pepper. Sauté for 1 minute.
3. Stir in the tomatoes, all the beans, the chili powder, chipotle powder, broth, and lime juice. Bring to a simmer. Cook, uncovered, for 15 minutes.
4. Taste and season with more salt and pepper, if desired. Top with the cashew cream and cheddar shreds.

Pro Tip: *This chili is mildly spicy. To turn down the heat, swap the chipotle powder for smoked paprika. The most important thing is to add that smokiness we love about chili.*

Per serving: Calories: 408; Total Fat: 5g; Saturated Fat: 1g; Trans Fat: 0g; Total Carbs: 71g; Fiber: 23g; Protein: 22g; Sodium: 2,191mg; Sugars: 11g

Roasted Butternut Squash Soup

SERVES 4

PREP TIME: 20 minutes

COOK TIME: 1 hour 15 minutes

Nothing evokes autumn like a creamy bowl of butternut squash soup. Variations of this warm, silky-smooth soup have been a fall tradition in my family for generations. This classic version is seasoned with my favorite autumn herbs—rosemary, thyme, sage, and oregano, which you'll find sprinkled throughout this book. This soup is a warm hug in a bowl.

GLUTEN-FREE, SOY-FREE

1 medium butternut squash, halved and seeded, skin on
2 tablespoons olive oil, divided
1 teaspoon salt
1 teaspoon black pepper
1 small yellow onion, diced
1 medium carrot, diced
1 celery stalk, diced
2 garlic cloves, roughly chopped
1 large russet potato, peeled and diced
½ teaspoon dried rosemary
½ teaspoon dried thyme
½ teaspoon dried sage
½ teaspoon dried oregano
6¼ cups vegetable broth
Cashew Cream (page 139)
Toasted pumpkin seeds

1. Preheat the oven to 350°F.
2. Brush the fleshy sides of the butternut squash with 1 tablespoon of the oil and season with salt and pepper. Place cut-side down in a large roasting pan.
3. Roast the squash for 25 minutes, until tender to the touch. The cut sides will be nicely browned and the flesh will be soft and scoopable. Remove from pan and set aside to cool.
4. Toss the onion, carrot, celery, and garlic into the roasting pan. Roast for 20 minutes, or until all the vegetables are tender.
5. Scoop the flesh from the squash halves. Discard the skin.
6. In a large soup pot over medium-high heat, heat the remaining 1 tablespoon of oil. Toss in all the roasted vegetables, and add the potato, rosemary, thyme, sage, and oregano.
7. Add the broth and bring to a boil. Cover the pot, reduce the heat, and simmer for 20 minutes.
8. Using an immersion blender, or transferring to a standard blender in small batches, puree the soup until smooth. Serve hot, garnished with cashew cream and pumpkin seeds.

Per serving: Calories: 235; Total Fat: 7g; Saturated Fat: 1g; Trans Fat: 0g; Total Carbs: 43g; Fiber: 8g; Protein: 4g; Sodium: 1,444mg; Sugars: 9g

Fun Fact: *Summertime watermelon is related to fall-favorite butternut squash—both are members of Cucurbitaceae. Of all the Cucurbitaceae siblings, butternut squash boasts the highest levels of vitamin A, an essential element for healthy eyes and our immune and reproductive systems.*

SERVES 4

PREP TIME:
10 minutes

COOK TIME:
15 minutes

Quick Cuban Black Bean Soup

Get carried away to Havana with this quick Cuban black bean soup. The silky soup calls for protein-packed black beans and just a handful of other ingredients. An easy and delicious soup on its own, it is also good over a bed of steamed rice and served with Pan-Sautéed Sweet Plantains (page 119).

30 MINUTES OR LESS, GLUTEN-FREE, ONE POT, SOY-FREE

2 tablespoons olive oil

1 large red onion, finely diced, divided

2 garlic cloves, minced

2 teaspoons ground cumin

2 (15-ounce) cans black beans, drained and rinsed, divided

2 cups vegetable broth

1 teaspoon red wine vinegar

¼ cup Cashew Cream (page 139)

¼ cup fresh cilantro, chopped

1. In a large soup pot over medium-high heat, heat the olive oil. Sauté half the onion for 3 to 5 minutes. Add the garlic and cumin, and sauté for 2 to 3 minutes.
2. Add 1 can of the beans and the broth. Bring to a boil, then remove from the heat.
3. Use an immersion blender to blend to a soupy consistency. Or let the beans cool a bit before transferring them to a conventional blender to puree, then return them to the pot.
4. Add the remaining can of beans, the other onion half, and the vinegar to the pot. Bring to a simmer.
5. Serve hot, garnished with cashew cream and cilantro.

Pro Tip: *Spruce up this simple recipe with a Cubanelle pepper—a long, sweet pepper you can find at most Caribbean and Latin markets. Seed and dice the pepper and sauté it with the onion.*

Per serving: Calories: 276; Total Fat: 9g; Saturated Fat: 1g; Trans Fat: 0g; Total Carbs: 37g; Fiber: 12g; Protein: 13g; Sodium: 306mg; Sugars: 3g

Hearty Vegetable Stew

SERVES 4

PREP TIME: 20 minutes

COOK TIME: 50 minutes

This robust stew is the perfect comfort meal to feed a hungry crowd. I love making it for holiday gatherings or when entertaining friends on a cold winter night. Slow-simmered in a fragrant broth with herbs, the tomatoes and velvety potatoes practically melt in your mouth. Make an extra batch and freeze for when you need to get a quick yet comforting meal on the table fast.

GLUTEN-FREE, NUT-FREE, ONE POT, SOY-FREE

- 2 tablespoons olive oil
- 1 small yellow onion, diced
- 2 large carrots, cut into ¼-inch-thick slices
- 2 celery stalks, cut into ¼-inch-thick slices
- ¼ teaspoon salt, plus more as needed
- 2 garlic cloves, minced
- 1 teaspoon dried rosemary
- 1 teaspoon dried thyme
- 1 teaspoon dried sage
- 1 teaspoon dried oregano
- 3 tablespoons rice flour
- ¼ cup dry red wine
- 4 cups vegetable broth
- 1 tablespoon tomato paste
- 1 (28-ounce) can whole peeled tomatoes with juice
- 4 small Yukon Gold or red potatoes, quartered
- ¼ teaspoon black pepper, plus more as needed
- 1 cup frozen peas
- 1 teaspoon red wine vinegar

1. In a large soup pot over medium-high heat, heat the olive oil. Sauté the onion, carrots, celery, and salt for 7 to 10 minutes, or until the onion is translucent.
2. Add the garlic, rosemary, thyme, sage, and oregano. Sauté for 1 to 2 minutes.
3. Stirring constantly, slowly add the rice flour to coat the vegetables. Sauté for 1 minute.
4. While stirring, slowly add the wine to deglaze the bottom and sides of the pot. Little by little, add the broth, stirring to break up any clumps.
5. Add the tomato paste, whole tomatoes with juice, potatoes, and pepper. Bring to a boil, then simmer, uncovered, for 25 to 30 minutes, or until the potatoes are tender.
6. Add the frozen peas and vinegar. Simmer for 5 minutes. Taste and season with salt and pepper. Serve immediately.

Pro Tip: *If you want an alcohol-free soup, use natural pomegranate or cranberry juice to deglaze the pot before adding the broth.*

Per serving: Calories: 334; Total Fat: 8g; Saturated Fat: 1g; Trans Fat: 0g; Total Carbs: 58g; Fiber: 10g; Protein: 8g; Sodium: 1,223mg; Sugars: 13g

Crispy Cauliflower Po' Boys, page 100

CHAPTER SEVEN

Burgers and Sandwiches

All-American Black Bean Burgers 92

Lentil Sloppy Joes 94

Portobello Steak and Chimichurri Sandwiches 95

Italian Seitan Sausage Hoagies 96

Grilled Vegetable Panini with Basil Pesto 97

Caribbean Island Burgers with Mango Relish 98

Jackfruit Barbecue Sandwiches 99

Crispy Cauliflower Po' Boys 100

Seared Oyster Mushroom Tortas 102

Tempeh BLTs 103

SERVES 4

PREP TIME: 15 minutes

COOK TIME: 30 minutes

All-American Black Bean Burgers

The humble black bean is the star of this all-American year-round favorite. Black beans are native to the Americas and are now a staple around the world, popular for their mild flavor and incredible versatility. For this recipe, we lightly roast the beans, which gives them that nice meaty bite we love about burgers. In place of chicken eggs, we use omega-3-loaded flax meal as our binder. And we pile our burgers high with all the classic fixin's.

NUT-FREE

FOR THE BURGERS

- 1½ cups canned black beans, drained, rinsed, and patted dry
- 3 tablespoons flax meal
- ⅓ cup warm water
- 1 (12-ounce) can diced fire-roasted tomatoes, drained
- 1 tablespoon garlic powder
- 1 tablespoon onion powder
- 1 tablespoon smoked paprika
- 1 teaspoon cumin powder
- 1 teaspoon salt, plus more as needed
- 1 teaspoon black pepper
- 1 cup vegan panko bread crumbs
- Vegetable oil spray
- 4 vegan American-style cheese slices

FOR SERVING (OPTIONAL)

- 4 vegan burger buns, split and toasted
- Romaine lettuce leaves
- Tomato slices
- Red onion slices
- Dill pickle slices
- Yellow mustard
- Aquafaba Mayo (page 141) or store-bought vegan mayo
- Ketchup

1. **Make the burgers:** Preheat the oven to 350°F. Line a baking sheet with parchment paper.
2. Spread the black beans evenly on the baking sheet and roast for 15 minutes. Let cool for 5 minutes.
3. In a small bowl, whisk together the flax meal and warm water to form a flax egg.
4. In a food processor, combine the roasted beans, flax egg, tomatoes, garlic powder, onion powder, smoked paprika, cumin powder, salt, and pepper. Pulse until mashed. Fold in the bread crumbs and then form the bean mixture into 4 large patties.

5. Heat a griddle or skillet over medium-high heat and lightly spray with the oil spray. Place the patties on the griddle and cook for 5 to 7 minutes. Flip them and top with the cheese slices. Cover the griddle lightly with foil and cook the patties for 5 to 7 minutes more to melt the cheese.

6. **Assemble the burgers:** Serve the burgers hot on buns or lettuce leaves, along with your garnishes of choice.

Pro Tip: *This patty mixture can be made ahead and kept refrigerated in an airtight container for up to 5 days. To freeze for up to 3 months, store the patties individually in small freezer bags. Thaw for 1 hour before cooking.*

Per serving: Calories: 550; Total Fat: 23g; Saturated Fat: 2g; Trans Fat: 0g; Total Carbs: 70g; Fiber: 14g; Protein: 18g; Sodium: 1,154mg; Sugars: 3g

SERVES 4

PREP TIME: 15 minutes

COOK TIME: 15 minutes

Lentil Sloppy Joes

Certain meals conjure fond memories of riding go-karts, playing Atari, and sporting questionable '80s hairstyles (which I'm only slightly ashamed of). Sloppy joes are at the top of that list! My brother, Michael, and I grew up in a house with two busy working parents where dinner was usually a one-pot special, and I was always excited when it was sloppy joes. This vegan version showcases heart-healthy lentils, and it's easy to make.

30 MINUTES OR LESS, NUT-FREE, ONE POT

- 1 tablespoon vegetable oil
- ½ small yellow onion, minced
- 2 garlic cloves, minced
- ¼ teaspoon salt, plus more as needed
- 1 (15-ounce) can tomato sauce
- ½ cup ketchup
- 2 tablespoons dark brown sugar, plus more as needed
- 2 tablespoons vegan Worcestershire sauce or steak sauce
- 1 teaspoon yellow mustard
- ¼ teaspoon onion powder
- ¼ teaspoon smoked paprika
- ¼ teaspoon black pepper
- 2 cups canned brown or green lentils, drained and rinsed (see Pro Tip)
- 4 vegan burger buns, split and toasted
- 8 dill pickle slices

1. In a medium soup pot over medium-high heat, heat the oil. Sauté the onion, garlic, and salt for 3 to 5 minutes. Stir in the tomato sauce, ketchup, brown sugar, Worcestershire sauce, mustard, onion powder, smoked paprika, and pepper.
2. Fold in the lentils. Simmer for 5 to 7 minutes until hot. Taste and season with more salt, if needed.
3. Fill the buns with the sloppy joe mix and top with pickle slices.

Pro Tip: *If cooking your own lentils, those cooked al dente work best for this recipe. You can also find canned lentils with the perfect texture at certain grocers, like Trader Joe's and Smart & Final.*

Per serving: Calories: 342; Total Fat: 6g; Saturated Fat: 0g; Trans Fat: 0g; Total Carbs: 62g; Fiber: 10g; Protein: 14g; Sodium: 1,471mg; Sugars: 19g

Portobello Steak and Chimichurri Sandwiches

PREP TIME:
10 minutes, plus
20 minutes
to marinate

COOK TIME:
10 minutes

These no-frills sandwiches are my ode to Argentina. On my first trip to Buenos Aires, I learned that, like Texas, Argentina is serious about its meat. In fact, this sandwich in its traditional form contains only three ingredients: beef, bread, and chimichurri sauce. For this modernized, eco-friendly version, we grill antioxidant-rich portobello mushrooms in place of carbon-footprint-heavy beef. Don't cry for me, Argentina—these mushrooms are meaty and delicious.

NUT-FREE

- 2 tablespoons canola oil
- 1 tablespoon tamari
- 1 tablespoon smoked paprika
- 1 teaspoon garlic powder
- 1 teaspoon onion powder
- ½ teaspoon ground cumin
- ¼ teaspoon black pepper
- 4 large portobello mushrooms, stems and gills removed
- 4 vegan hoagie rolls, split and toasted
- 1 recipe Chimichurri Sauce (page 140) or 2 cups store-bought chimichurri sauce

1. In a small bowl, whisk together the oil, tamari, smoked paprika, garlic powder, onion powder, cumin, and pepper.
2. Place the mushroom caps on a large plate or in a medium shallow pan and evenly coat with the marinade. Let marinate for 20 minutes.
3. Preheat a grill to medium-high heat.
4. Grill the mushrooms for 4 to 5 minutes per side over a direct flame until nicely charred. Remove from the heat and cut into ½-inch strips.
5. Fill each roll with some portobello slices and drizzle with the chimichurri.

Pro Tip: *No grill available? Preheat a cast-iron skillet over medium-high heat. Add the marinated mushrooms and press them down with a second cast-iron skillet or a grill press. Sear for 4 to 5 minutes per side. The skillet handle will be very hot, so wear heat-resistant gloves.*

Per serving: Calories: 400; Total Fat: 22g; Saturated Fat: 3g; Trans Fat: 0g; Total Carbs: 45g; Fiber: 3g; Protein: 9g; Sodium: 782mg; Sugars: 7g

SERVES 4

PREP TIME:
10 minutes

COOK TIME:
20 minutes

Italian Seitan Sausage Hoagies

This plant-based take on the classic Italian-American street food features our seitan-based Italian Sausage. This scrumptious sandwich is big and beautiful—perfect for a robust lunch or dinner.

30 MINUTES OR LESS, NUT-FREE, ONE POT

- **2 tablespoons olive oil**
- **1 recipe Italian Sausage (page 108) or 4 links store-bought plant-based Italian sausage, cut diagonally into ½-inch slices**
- **1 small yellow onion, julienned**
- **1 medium red bell pepper, julienned**
- **¼ teaspoon salt**
- **1 cup 20-Minute Marinara (page 132) or store-bought marinara**
- **½ cup shredded vegan mozzarella**
- **4 (8-inch) vegan hoagie rolls, split and toasted**

1. Heat a large skillet over medium-high heat. Add the olive oil and sauté the sausage for 3 to 5 minutes, until nicely browned.
2. Add the onion, bell pepper, and salt. Sauté for 3 to 5 minutes, stirring occasionally, until the onion is browned.
3. Stir in the marinara and mozzarella and heat until the cheese melts.
4. Fill each roll with some sausage, onion, bell pepper, and marinara mix.

Pro Tip: *Mix things up by using any of our Seitan Sausage 3 Ways recipes (page 106). The Spanish Chorizo will add a little smokiness to the hoagie, while the Apple-Sage Andouille Sausage will add a hint of heat and sweetness.*

Per serving: Calories: 684; Total Fat: 19g; Saturated Fat: 4g; Trans Fat: 0g; Total Carbs: 75g; Fiber: 8g; Protein: 56g; Sodium: 1,600mg; Sugars: 7g

Grilled Vegetable Panini with Basil Pesto

SERVES 4

PREP TIME: 10 minutes

COOK TIME: 20 minutes

Zucchini, eggplant, portobellos, and red bell peppers come together to create this over-the-top all-veggie sandwich. Chargrilled to perfection, the seasoned veggies are layered on Basil Pesto–lathered sourdough. Even the most notorious vegetable hater will love this veggie all-star!

30 MINUTES OR LESS

3 tablespoons olive oil, divided

½ teaspoon garlic powder

½ teaspoon onion powder

½ teaspoon dried oregano

½ teaspoon salt

¼ teaspoon black pepper

1 medium zucchini, thinly sliced on a diagonal

1 small eggplant, thinly sliced on a diagonal

2 portobello mushroom caps, stems and gills removed, caps cut into 1-inch slices

2 red bell peppers, quartered

¼ cup Basil Pesto (page 133) or store-bought vegan pesto

8 slices vegan sourdough bread

½ cup shredded vegan mozzarella, plus more as needed

1. In a small bowl, whisk 2 tablespoons of olive oil with the garlic powder, onion powder, oregano, salt, and pepper. Lightly coat the zucchini, eggplant, mushroom caps, and bell peppers with the spice rub.
2. Heat a large grill pan or skillet over high heat. Grill the vegetables for 3 to 7 minutes per side, until they have a nice char. Keep the grill hot.
3. Spread 1 tablespoon of the pesto on one side of 4 bread slices. Top with 1 tablespoon of mozzarella shreds, then evenly distribute and layer the vegetables atop the cheese.
4. Top the vegetables with 1 tablespoon each of mozzarella shreds. Place the remaining 4 bread slices atop to close the sandwiches.
5. Lightly brush both sides of the sandwiches with the remaining tablespoon of oil. Grill the sandwiches for 2 to 3 minutes per side, until the cheese melts and the bread is crispy.

Per serving: Calories: 661; Total Fat: 26g; Saturated Fat: 3g; Trans Fat: 0g; Total Carbs: 89g; Fiber: 12g; Protein: 20g; Sodium: 1,225mg; Sugars: 10g

Origin story: *When I began my vegan journey, one of the first takeout meals I had was a basic grilled vegetable panini. Back then, restaurants typically didn't carry vegan cheese or make vegan-friendly sauces, so I had the server omit the mozzarella and pesto. This fully realized iteration doesn't require you to miss out on anything.*

SERVES 4

PREP TIME: 15 minutes

COOK TIME: 30 minutes

Caribbean Island Burgers with Mango Relish

These sweet and savory burgers are what Caribbean dreams are made of. I created this recipe on a trip to the beautiful island of Puerto Rico, where I was inspired by its lush landscapes and abundance of tropical fruits.

NUT-FREE

1½ cups canned red beans, drained, rinsed, and patted dry

1 teaspoon vegetable oil, plus more for cooking

1 small red onion, one half diced small, one half cut into rings (for topping)

1 garlic clove, minced

1 medium-ripe plantain, cubed (see Pro Tip)

½ cup quick oats

1 teaspoon ground cumin

1 to 2 teaspoons salt

¼ teaspoon black pepper

4 large vegan burger buns, split and toasted

¼ cup Aquafaba Mayo (page 141) or store-bought vegan mayo

1 cup Mango Relish (page 138)

1 Hass avocado, sliced into wedges

1. Preheat the oven to 350°F. Line a baking sheet with parchment paper.
2. Spread the beans evenly on the baking sheet and roast for 15 minutes. Let cool briefly.
3. In a large pan over medium-high heat, heat the oil. Add the diced onion and garlic and sauté for 3 to 5 minutes, stirring occasionally.
4. Add the plantain and sauté for 2 to 3 minutes, stirring, until mostly tender.
5. Add the roasted beans, oats, cumin, salt, and pepper. Using a potato masher, combine well. Remove from the heat and let cool.
6. Lightly oil a large nonstick skillet and heat over medium-high heat.
7. Form the bean mixture into 4 patties. Cook for 4 to 6 minutes per side, until nicely browned.
8. Spread each bun with some mayo, add a patty, and top with an onion ring, the mango relish, and avocado wedges.

Per serving: Calories: 585; Total Fat: 22g; Saturated Fat: 2g; Trans Fat: 0g; Total Carbs: 88g; Fiber: 13g; Protein: 15g; Sodium: 1,236mg; Sugars: 26g

Pro Tip: *Plantains are ripe when their skins are yellow, with dark patchy areas. Green plantains are starchier and won't work for this recipe. And overly ripe plantains with more dark patchy areas than yellow will make mushy patties.*

Jackfruit Barbecue Sandwiches

SERVES 4

PREP TIME: 10 minutes

COOK TIME: 30 minutes

Summer family road trips always included stops at the most raved-about barbecue joints across the Lone Star State. My go-to menu selection was the shredded barbecue sandwich. I loved the delicate texture and that smoky sauce dripping off the bun. Like any respectable Texan, I still love a good ol' sloppy barbecue sandwich, but now, I enjoy it in a meat-free way! Young jackfruit—also colloquially called "vegan pulled pork"—is our meaty vehicle of choice here for the smoky barbecue sauce.

NUT-FREE, ONE POT

1 tablespoon vegetable oil

½ small yellow onion, julienned

¼ teaspoon salt

1 (14-ounce) can young jackfruit, drained, patted dry or pressed to remove excess fluid, and shredded

1 recipe Texas-Style Barbecue Sauce (page 134) or 4 cups store-bought barbecue sauce

4 large vegan burger buns, split and toasted

¼ cup Aquafaba Mayo (page 141) or store-bought vegan mayo

8 dill pickle slices

1. In a large skillet over medium-high heat, heat the oil. Add the onion and salt. Sauté for 3 to 4 minutes, until the onion is translucent.
2. Add the jackfruit. Sauté for 5 to 7 minutes, stirring occasionally, until nicely browned.
3. Stir in the barbecue sauce and simmer, uncovered, for about 15 minutes, until the sauce is reduced by about half.
4. Spread the cut side of each bun with some mayo. To the bottom half of each bun, add the barbecue jackfruit and top with dill pickle slices. Place the remaining bun halves on top to close the sandwiches.

Pro Tip: *When buying jackfruit for this recipe, look for young jackfruit, sometimes labeled "green jackfruit." Large yellow jackfruit is fully ripened and too sweet.*

Per serving: Calories: 502; Total Fat: 21g; Saturated Fat: 1.4g; Trans Fat: 0g; Total Carbs: 78g; Fiber: 3g; Protein: 5g; Sodium: 1,240mg; Sugars: 24g

SERVES 4

PREP TIME: 25 minutes

COOK TIME: 25 minutes

Crispy Cauliflower Po' Boys

Oven-crisped cauliflower steps in for seafood in this New Orleans original. Our secret ingredient is dulse seaweed, which adds a delicate seafood taste. We take our po' boys up a notch with slightly spicy plant-based rémoulade sauce (so delish), which can be replaced with the more traditional (vegan) mayo to save time, if you like. These po' boys are a real crowd-pleaser!

NUT-FREE

FOR THE RÉMOULADE SAUCE

- ½ cup Aquafaba Mayo (page 141) or store-bought vegan mayo
- 1 garlic clove, minced
- 1 tablespoon dill pickle relish
- 1 teaspoon Louisiana hot sauce
- 1 teaspoon drained capers, minced
- ½ teaspoon paprika
- ½ teaspoon Dijon mustard
- ½ teaspoon vegan Worcestershire sauce or steak sauce
- Juice of ½ small lime

FOR THE CRISPY CAULIFLOWER

- 3 tablespoons flax meal
- ½ cup water
- 1 large head cauliflower, cut into bite-sized florets (about 6 cups)
- 2 cups vegan panko bread crumbs
- 1 teaspoon dulse seaweed flakes
- Vegetable oil spray
- Salt

FOR THE PO' BOYS

- 4 (8-inch) vegan French baguettes, split horizontally
- 2 cups shredded iceberg lettuce
- 8 to 12 slices Roma (plum) tomato
- 16 dill pickle slices
- Louisiana hot sauce

1. **Make the rémoulade:** In a medium bowl, whisk together the mayo, garlic, relish, hot sauce, capers, paprika, mustard, Worcestershire sauce, and lime juice. Chill until ready to use.
2. **Make the crispy cauliflower:** Preheat the oven to 400°F. Line a large baking sheet with parchment paper. (See Pro Tip.)
3. In a large bowl, whisk together the flax meal and water. Add the cauliflower and stir to coat well.
4. In another large bowl, whisk together the panko and dulse. Add the cauliflower and toss together. Evenly spread the cauliflower on the baking sheet and lightly coat with oil spray.

5. Roast for 20 to 25 minutes, until crispy. Season with salt.

6. **Assemble the po' boys:** Spread the cut sides of the halved baguettes with the rémoulade. Add the lettuce and tomato slices to the bottom halves.

7. Arrange the crispy cauliflower on top and add the pickle slices. Drizzle with hot sauce. Place the remaining bread halves on top to close the sandwiches.

Pro Tip: *This recipe works well in an air fryer. At 400°F, air-fry the florets in small batches for 20 minutes, shaking the basket halfway through. Season the air-fried florets with salt.*

Per serving: Calories: 1,254; Total Fat: 44g; Saturated Fat: 4g; Trans Fat: 1g; Total Carbs: 190g; Fiber: 17g; Protein: 33g; Sodium: 2,939mg; Sugars: 18g

SERVES 4

PREP TIME:
15 minutes, plus
20 minutes
to marinate

COOK TIME:
15 minutes

Seared Oyster Mushroom Tortas

With their mild taste and silky texture, oyster mushrooms are the perfect fungi to mimic chicken. We marinate our hearty mushrooms with a simple spice rub, then sear them to bring out their naturally meaty qualities.

NUT-FREE, SOY-FREE

- 1 tablespoon olive oil
- 1 teaspoon dark chili powder
- 1 teaspoon garlic powder
- 1 teaspoon black pepper
- 1 teaspoon salt
- ½ teaspoon onion powder
- 1 pound fresh oyster mushrooms
- 4 vegan bolillos or hoagie rolls, split and toasted
- ¼ cup Aquafaba Mayo (page 141) or store-bought vegan mayo
- 1 cup shredded iceberg lettuce
- 8 slices ripe Roma (plum) tomato
- ½ cup Easy Guacamole (page 111) or store-bought guacamole
- 2 tablespoons chopped fresh cilantro

1. In a large bowl, whisk together the olive oil, chili powder, garlic powder, pepper, salt, and onion powder to form a thick paste. Rub the paste into the mushrooms and let marinate for 20 minutes.
2. Heat a cast-iron skillet over medium-high heat. Add the mushrooms and any remaining seasoning. Press down on the mushrooms with a second cast-iron skillet or a grill press. (The handles will be hot, so wear heat-resistant gloves and be careful not to burn yourself.) Sear the mushrooms for 4 to 5 minutes, then flip and sear on the other side for another 4 minutes.
3. Reduce the heat to medium and cook the mushrooms for 4 to 5 minutes more, stirring occasionally. Remove the mushrooms from the skillet and let cool for 2 to 3 minutes. When cool enough to handle, slice the mushroom clusters into bite-sized pieces.
4. Spread both sides of the bolillos with some mayo. Add the mushrooms and top with the lettuce, tomato slices, guacamole, and cilantro. Place the remaining bolillo halves on top to close the sandwiches.

Pro Tip: *This method of searing mushrooms can create a lot of smoke. Make sure there's plenty of ventilation—especially if you live in a small space.*

Per serving: Calories: 413; Total Fat: 21g; Saturated Fat: 2g; Trans Fat: 0g; Total Carbs: 50g; Fiber: 7g; Protein: 11g; Sodium: 1,072mg; Sugars: 7g

Tempeh BLTs

SERVES 4

PREP TIME:
10 minutes

COOK TIME:
5 minutes

Sometimes it's the simple things vegans miss most. Like a modest BLT. But not anymore! Tempeh saves the day in this updated version of the family favorite. The secret to making a great tempeh BLT is to layer it with fresh, crisp lettuce and perfectly sun-ripened tomatoes. Tangy Aquafaba Mayo seals the deal.

30 MINUTES OR LESS, NUT-FREE, ONE POT

8 slices vegan bread of choice

½ cup Aquafaba Mayo (page 141) or store-bought vegan mayo

8 crisp iceberg lettuce leaves

8 (¼-inch-thick) slices ripe beefsteak or heirloom tomato

1 recipe Tempeh Bacon (page 120)

1. Toast the bread.
2. Spread each slice of toast with 1 tablespoon of the mayo.
3. Place 1 lettuce leaf each atop 4 pieces of toast.
4. Place 2 tomato slices each atop the lettuce leaves.
5. Evenly divide the tempeh bacon and place atop the tomato slices.
6. Place 1 lettuce leaf each atop the bacon.
7. Place the remaining 4 toast pieces atop the lettuce to close the sandwiches.

Pro Tip: *To add zing to your BLT, whisk 1 to 2 teaspoons sriracha into the mayo. To sweeten things, add 1 tablespoon yellow mustard plus 1 tablespoon agave nectar to the mayo.*

Per serving: Calories: 535; Total Fat: 38g; Saturated Fat: 4g; Trans Fat: 0g; Total Carbs: 34g; Fiber: 6g; Protein: 19g; Sodium: 911mg; Sugars: 7g

Crostini with Macadamia Ricotta, Strawberries, and Basil, page 110

CHAPTER EIGHT

Apps, Sides, and Snacks

Seitan Sausage 3 Ways
- Spanish Chorizo **106**
- Italian Sausage **108**
- Apple-Sage Andouille Sausages **109**

Crostini with Macadamia Ricotta, Strawberries, and Basil **110**

Easy Guacamole **111**

Cashew Mozzarella and Marinara Dip **112**

Tofu Summer Rolls **113**

Italian-Herbed Roasted Chickpeas **114**

Baked Barbecue Cauliflower Wings **115**

Grilled Tofu and Veggie Kabobs with Chimichurri Sauce **116**

Broccoli with Butternut Squash Cheese Sauce **117**

Oven Home Fries **118**

Pan-Sautéed Sweet Plantains **119**

Tempeh Bacon **120**

Rustic Roasted Root Vegetables **121**

Spanish Rice **122**

Refried Pintos **123**

Seitan Sausage 3 Ways

Charcuterie night is back, thanks to our seitan sausage trio. This collection—made from a base of beans and vital wheat gluten—features smoky Spanish chorizo, Italian-herbed sausage, and spicy New Orleans-style Andouille sausage. They show up in recipes as varied as the Spanish Chorizo and Vegetable Paella (page 164), Pasta Bolognese (page 145), and Seitan Sausage Jambalaya (page 159).

Making sausage is time-consuming, and the ingredients lists can look long (there's nothing exotic here), but it's wise to make these recipes in large batches as part of a meal-prep session and freeze them until ready to use. You'll have the basis for multiple meals at the ready.

MAKES
4 sausages

PREP TIME:
20 minutes

COOK TIME:
45 minutes

Spanish Chorizo

NUT-FEE, SOY-FREE

1 tablespoon toasted sesame oil
¼ medium yellow onion, minced
¼ red bell pepper, minced
2 garlic cloves, minced
1 tablespoon finely chopped fresh parsley
⅓ cup canned white beans, drained, rinsed, and mashed well with a fork
½ teaspoon red wine vinegar
1 cup vital wheat gluten
2 tablespoons nutritional yeast
1 tablespoon ground cumin
1 tablespoon smoked paprika
1 teaspoon dried thyme
1 teaspoon salt
½ teaspoon onion powder
½ teaspoon black pepper
¼ teaspoon sugar
1 cup vegetable broth
Vegetable oil spray

1. In a large pan over medium heat, heat the oil. Sauté the onion, bell pepper, and garlic for 5 minutes. Add the parsley, beans, and vinegar. Heat through, then remove from the heat.
2. In a large bowl, whisk together the gluten, nutritional yeast, cumin, smoked paprika, thyme, salt, onion powder, pepper, and sugar. Fold in the bean mixture. Pour in the broth and mix well with your hands, mashing and kneading the dough 5 or 6 times. Spread the dough on a cutting board and cut into 4 equal pieces.
3. Lightly spray 4 pieces of 8-by-6-inch aluminum foil with the oil spray.
4. Roll a piece of dough in your hand and shape it into a 6-inch-long, 1-inch-thick sausage. Place the sausage in a foil wrapper, roll the foil around the sausage, twist the ends, and fold them in so it is tightly wrapped. (The sausages will swell when they cook.) Repeat to make 3 more sausages.
5. Put about 2 inches of water in a large, deep pot. Add a steamer basket, making sure the water line is below the basket. Place the sausages in a row in the steamer basket; if you need more room, stack them at right angles, like logs on a fire. Cover and steam for 40 to 45 minutes, adding more water to the pot as needed.
6. Remove the steamer basket from the heat and let the sausages cool. When cool enough to touch, unwrap the sausages.

Per serving (1 sausage): Calories: 286; Total Fat: 5g; Saturated Fat: 1g; Trans Fat: 0g; Total Carbs: 16g; Fiber: 3g; Protein: 46g; Sodium: 46mg; Sugars: 1g

CONTINUED

Italian Sausage

NUT-FREE, SOY-FREE

MAKES
4 sausages

PREP TIME:
20 minutes

COOK TIME:
45 minutes

1 tablespoon olive oil
¼ medium yellow onion, minced
2 garlic cloves, minced
1 tablespoon fennel seeds
2 tablespoons minced oil-packed sun-dried tomatoes
⅓ cup canned white beans, drained, rinsed, and mashed well with a fork
1 tablespoon finely chopped fresh parsley
½ teaspoon red wine vinegar
1 cup vital wheat gluten
2 tablespoons nutritional yeast
1 teaspoon ground cumin
1 teaspoon dried oregano
1 teaspoon dried thyme
1 teaspoon dried basil
1 teaspoon dried sage
1 teaspoon salt
½ teaspoon black pepper
¼ teaspoon sugar
1 cup vegetable broth
Vegetable oil spray

1. In a large pan over medium heat, heat the olive oil. Sauté the onion, garlic, and fennel seeds for 5 minutes. Add the sun-dried tomatoes, mashed beans, parsley, and vinegar. Heat through, then remove from the heat.
2. In a large bowl, whisk together the gluten, nutritional yeast, cumin, oregano, thyme, basil, sage, salt, pepper, and sugar. Fold in the bean mixture. Pour in the broth and mix well with your hands, mashing and kneading the dough 5 or 6 times. Spread the dough on a cutting board and cut into 4 equal pieces.
3. Lightly spray 4 pieces of 8-by-6-inch aluminum foil with the oil spray.
4. Roll a piece of dough in your hand and shape into a 6-inch-long, 1-inch-thick sausage. Place the sausage in a foil wrapper, roll the foil around the sausage, twist the ends, and fold them in so it is tightly wrapped. (They swell when they cook.) Repeat to make 3 more sausages.
5. Put about 2 inches of water in a large, deep pot. Add a steamer basket, making sure the water line is below the basket. Place the sausages in a row in the steamer basket; if you need more room, stack them at right angles, like logs on a fire. Cover and steam for 40 to 45 minutes, adding more water to the pot as needed.
6. Remove the steamer basket from the heat and let the sausages cool. When cool enough to touch, unwrap the sausages.

Per serving (1 sausage): Calories: 296; Total Fat: 5g; Saturated Fat: 1g; Trans Fat: 0g; Total Carbs: 17g; Fiber: 3g; Protein: 46g; Sodium: 743mg; Sugars: 1g

Apple-Sage Andouille Sausage

MAKES
4 sausages

PREP TIME:
20 minutes

COOK TIME:
45 minutes

NUT-FREE

1 tablespoon toasted sesame oil
¼ medium yellow onion, minced
2 garlic cloves, minced
½ green apple, cored, peeled, and minced
⅓ cup canned red kidney beans, drained, rinsed, and mashed well with a fork
1 tablespoon tomato paste
½ teaspoon red wine vinegar
½ teaspoon liquid smoke
1 tablespoon soy sauce
1 teaspoon maple syrup
1 cup vital wheat gluten
2 tablespoons nutritional yeast
1 teaspoon salt
1 teaspoon dried sage
1 teaspoon smoked paprika
1 teaspoon sweet paprika
½ teaspoon dried thyme
½ teaspoon red pepper flakes
¼ teaspoon cayenne pepper
¼ teaspoon black pepper
1 cup vegetable broth
Vegetable oil spray

1. In a large pan over medium heat, heat the oil. Sauté the onion, garlic, and apple for 5 minutes. Add the mashed beans, tomato paste, vinegar, liquid smoke, soy sauce, and maple syrup. Heat through, then remove from the heat.
2. In a large bowl, whisk together the gluten, nutritional yeast, salt, sage, paprikas, thyme, red pepper flakes, cayenne, and pepper. Fold in the bean mixture. Pour in the broth and mix well with your hands, mashing and kneading the dough 5 or 6 times. Spread the dough on a cutting board and cut into 4 equal pieces.
3. Lightly spray 4 pieces of 8-by-6-inch aluminum foil with oil spray.
4. Roll a piece of dough in your hand and shape into a 6-inch-long, 1-inch-thick sausage. Place the sausage in a foil wrapper, roll the foil around the sausage, twist the ends, and fold them in so it is tightly wrapped. (They swell when they cook.) Repeat to make 3 more sausages.
5. Put about 2 inches of water in a large, deep pot. Add a steamer basket, making sure the water line is below the basket. Place the sausages in a row in the steamer basket; if you need more room, stack them at right angles, like logs on a fire.
6. Cover and steam for 40 to 45 minutes, adding more water to the pot as needed.
7. Remove the steamer basket from the heat and let the sausages cool. When cool enough to touch, unwrap the sausages.

Per serving (1 sausage): Calories: 300; Total Fat: 5g; Saturated Fat: 1g; Trans Fat: 0g; Total Carbs: 19g; Fiber: 3g; Protein: 47g; Sodium: 1,016mg; Sugars: 4g

Pro Tip: *This recipe trio was designed to give you the basic skills and formula to become a vegan sausage master. Get creative and mix things up with different herbs and spices.*

SERVES 4

PREP TIME: 10 minutes

COOK TIME: 20 minutes

Crostini with Macadamia Ricotta, Strawberries, and Basil

These crostini are a perfect appetizer for any Italian meal. I developed this recipe as an hors d'oeuvre for the Humane Society of the United States' 2019 "To the Rescue!" gala at Cipriani restaurant in New York City. It was one of the most raved-about and easy-to-make starters, so I wanted to share it.

30 MINUTES OR LESS, SOY-FREE

¼ vegan French baguette, cut into 8 (¼-inch) slices

1 to 2 tablespoons olive oil

½ teaspoon salt, plus more for seasoning

Black pepper

1 cup raw unsalted macadamia nuts

1 teaspoon fresh lemon juice

¼ cup water, plus more as needed

3 or 4 fresh strawberries, hulled and thinly sliced

¼ cup Balsamic Reduction (page 137)

8 fresh basil leaves

1. Preheat the oven to 350°F. Arrange the baguette slices on a small baking sheet. Brush both sides with the olive oil and season with the salt and pepper.
2. Bake for 15 to 20 minutes, until golden brown. Let cool on the baking sheet.
3. In a food processor, combine the macadamias, lemon juice, ½ teaspoon salt, and ¼ cup water. Process until smooth, scraping down the sides and adding more water as necessary.
4. Generously spread the macadamia "ricotta" on the crostini. Top each with 3 strawberry slices. Drizzle each with the balsamic reduction and garnish with the basil.

Pro Tip: *No macadamia nuts? Use Brazil nuts. To remove their skins, submerge the nuts in an ice bath for 5 to 10 minutes, then peel.*

Per serving: Calories: 357; Total Fat: 31g; Saturated Fat: 5g; Trans Fat: 0g; Total Carbs: 19g; Fiber: 3g; Protein: 4g; Sodium: 390mg; Sugars: 8g

Easy Guacamole

SERVES 4

PREP TIME:
10 minutes

Stop paying for overpriced packaged guacamole and make your own instead. All you need are a few simple ingredients and you'll be snacking on super-fresh guac in no time. Serve this alongside any Tex-Mex dish. Heck, even pile it onto your favorite burger or sandwich for some flair!

30 MINUTES OR LESS, GLUTEN-FREE, NUT-FREE, OIL-FREE, ONE POT, SOY-FREE

3 ripe Hass avocados

1 cup Salsa Fresca (page 130) or store-bought fresh red salsa

Salt

1. In a large bowl, mash the avocados until they are mostly creamy, leaving some chunks.
2. Stir in the salsa and combine well. Taste and season with salt.

Shopping Tip: *It's important to think ahead when buying avocados. To pick avocados for today, choose those that are slightly soft when gently squeezed. If planning to eat them 3 to 4 days from now, choose those that are mostly green and hard but starting to darken.*

Per serving: Calories: 184; Total Fat: 16g; Saturated Fat: 2g; Trans Fat: 0g; Total Carbs: 12g; Fiber: 8g; Protein: 3g; Sodium: 83mg; Sugars: 2g

SERVES 4

PREP TIME:
10 minutes, plus
20 minutes to soak

COOK TIME:
5 minutes

Cashew Mozzarella and Marinara Dip

A childhood favorite is reimagined with this creamy, tomatoey dip. Tapioca flour is the secret to turning the milky cashew mix into a gooey, mozzarella-style cheese dip. Top the dip with 20-Minute Marinara for a scrumptious starter the whole table will be fighting for.

GLUTEN-FREE

- ½ cup raw unsalted cashews, soaked in hot water for 20 minutes, drained, and rinsed
- 1 cup water
- 3 tablespoons tapioca starch
- ½ teaspoon nutritional yeast
- Juice of ½ lemon
- ½ teaspoon salt
- ¼ teaspoon garlic powder
- ¼ teaspoon onion powder
- Pinch of white pepper or black pepper
- 1 cup 20-Minute Marinara (page 132) or store-bought marinara, heated
- 1 to 2 tablespoons Basil Pesto (page 133) or store-bought vegan pesto (optional)
- ½ vegan French baguette, cut into ½-inch slices and toasted

1. In a large blender, combine the cashews, water, tapioca starch, nutritional yeast, lemon juice, salt, garlic powder, onion powder, and white pepper. Blend on high speed until very smooth.
2. Pour the mixture into a small saucepan and cook over medium-high heat for about 5 minutes, stirring consistently with a wooden spoon. The cheese should become nice and stretchy.
3. Transfer the cheese to a large bowl and top with warmed marinara. Top with the pesto, if desired. Serve hot with toasted baguette slices for dipping.

Pro Tip: *If you don't want to make all 4 servings right away, cook part of the milky cashew mix. The remainder can be refrigerated in a sealed container for up to 5 days.*

Per serving: Calories: 228; Total Fat: 9g; Saturated Fat: 2g; Trans Fat: 0g; Total Carbs: 31g; Fiber: 2g; Protein: 8g; Sodium: 605mg; Sugars: 5g

Tofu Summer Rolls

MAKES
8 summer rolls

PREP TIME:
20 minutes

COOK TIME:
20 minutes

There are a few tricks that make this recipe foolproof: We soak the noodles in hot water instead of cooking them to prevent overcooking. We have all the ingredients prepped and the workplace cleared before rolling the rice papers. Lastly, we use damp hands to roll the summer rolls to prevent sticking and tearing. Make these with friends or fam for a fun premeal activity!

GLUTEN-FREE

- 4 ounces rice vermicelli noodles
- 1 teaspoon vegetable oil
- 8 ounces extra-firm tofu, drained, pressed, cut into 8 even slabs
- 1 recipe Peanut Sauce (page 131) or 1 cup store-bought sauce, divided
- 1 red bell pepper, julienned
- 1 medium carrot, julienned
- 1 small cucumber, peeled and julienned
- ¼ cup fresh cilantro, stemmed
- ¼ cup fresh mint, stemmed
- 8 rice paper wrappers, plus more as needed

1. Bring a medium pot of water to a boil, then remove from the heat. Submerge the noodles in the water and let soak for 3 to 5 minutes, until tender. Drain in a colander and set aside.
2. In a skillet over medium-high heat, heat the oil. Sear the tofu slabs for 3 minutes. Flip the slabs and glaze each with some peanut sauce. Cook for 3 minutes, flip the slabs again, and glaze the other side. Flip again, then remove from the heat.
3. Before assembling the rolls, divide the noodles, julienned bell pepper, carrot, and cucumber, cilantro, and mint into 8 equal portions.
4. Pour some hot water into a large, shallow pan. Submerge 1 rice paper wrapper in the water and let soften for 10 to 15 seconds.
5. Transfer the wrapper to a flat, damp surface and spread out into its full circular shape. At the bottom end of the wrapper, place 1 portion of vermicelli noodles, 1 portion of julienned vegetables, 1 portion of cilantro, 1 portion of mint, and 1 slab of tofu.
6. Using mildly damp hands, gently fold the filled part of the rice paper up to the center. Fold in the ends to seal the sides, then fold again to seal the roll completely. Place the roll on a plate, seam side down, and cover with a damp kitchen towel.
7. Repeat until all rolls have been filled. Serve immediately with the remaining peanut sauce to dip.

Per serving (2 rolls): Calories: 402; Total Fat: 20g; Saturated Fat: 4g; Trans Fat: 0g; Total Carbs: 45g; Fiber: 4g; Protein: 15g; Sodium: 825mg; Sugars: 16g

Pro Tip: *This recipe is typically made with raw tofu, but since I know many of y'all are new to tofu, I wanted to give it a little flavor before filling the rolls. If you prefer the traditional method, skip step 2.*

SERVES 4

PREP TIME:
10 minutes

COOK TIME:
40 minutes

Italian-Herbed Roasted Chickpeas

A favorite among the vegan bodybuilding set, chickpeas are one of the most versatile legumes on the planet. Here, chickpeas are turned into a crunchy, protein-packed snack you can tote in your gym bag. This recipe also serves as our substitute for boring croutons in Caesar Salad with Italian-Herbed Roasted Chickpeas (page 75). I suggest making these in large batches so you can snack on them anytime you feel munchy.

GLUTEN-FREE, NUT-FREE, SOY-FREE

1 (15-ounce) can chickpeas, drained, rinsed, and patted dry
1½ teaspoons olive oil
½ teaspoon garlic powder
½ teaspoon onion powder
½ teaspoon dried oregano
½ teaspoon dried rosemary
½ teaspoon dried thyme
¼ teaspoon dried sage
½ teaspoon salt
¼ teaspoon black pepper

1. Preheat the oven to 400°F. Line a baking sheet with parchment paper.
2. In a large bowl, toss together the chickpeas, olive oil, and seasonings and stir to evenly coat the chickpeas. Spread the seasoned chickpeas out on the baking sheet.
3. Roast for 30 to 40 minutes, stirring and turning the pan halfway through, until the chickpeas are crispy on the outside and still slightly tender inside. Let cool. Store them in an airtight container in a cool, dry place for a few days.

Pro Tip: *Use any combination of spices for variety. Instead of herbs, I sometimes mix my chickpeas with garam masala. Chili powder is excellent, too.*

Per serving: Calories: 116; Total Fat: 3g; Saturated Fat: 1g; Trans Fat: 0g; Total Carbs: 17g; Fiber: 5g; Protein: 6g; Sodium: 440mg; Sugars: 3g

Baked Barbecue Cauliflower Wings

SERVES 4

PREP TIME: 10 minutes

COOK TIME: 25 minutes

By now, you know I'm a sucker for anything barbecue. And these tangy wings really hit the spot when I'm looking for that Texas flavor on game night. Crispy on the outside and tender inside, the smoky wings scream, "Game on!"

NUT-FREE

3 tablespoons flax meal

½ cup water

1 large head cauliflower, cut into small florets (about 6 cups)

2 cups vegan panko bread crumbs

1 teaspoon garlic powder

1 teaspoon onion powder

1 teaspoon salt

½ teaspoon black pepper

Olive oil spray

1 recipe Texas-Style Barbecue Sauce (page 134) or 4 cups store-bought barbecue sauce

1. Preheat the oven to 400°F. Line a large baking sheet with parchment paper.
2. In a large bowl, whisk the flax meal and water. Add the cauliflower and coat well.
3. In another large bowl, whisk the panko, garlic powder, onion powder, salt, and pepper. Add the cauliflower and toss together. Spread the seasoned cauliflower on the baking sheet and coat with olive oil spray.
4. Roast for 20 to 25 minutes, until crispy.
5. Transfer to a large bowl and add the barbecue sauce. Gently toss to coat and serve hot on a large platter for everyone to share.

Pro Tip: *Kikkoman brand panko bread crumbs are vegan.*

Per serving: Calories: 648; Total Fat: 15g; Saturated Fat: 2g; Trans Fat: 0g; Total Carbs: 121g; Fiber: 9g; Protein: 12g; Sodium: 1,895mg; Sugars: 26g

MAKES
12 skewers

PREP TIME:
20 minutes, plus 30 minutes to marinate

COOK TIME:
10 minutes

Grilled Tofu and Veggie Kabobs with Chimichurri Sauce

When I was growing up, my dad was the grill master—he made sure everything was charred to perfection. But I helped build our kabobs and coat them in our wonderfully herby chimichurri sauce. In this recipe, I honor my dad with these vegan kabobs.

GLUTEN-FREE, NUT-FREE

8 cups water, divided

8 cups ice cubes, divided

12 broccoli florets

12 cauliflower florets

2 medium red onions, cut into 24 large pieces

2 red bell peppers, cut into 12 pieces

1 pound extra-firm tofu, drained, pressed, and cut into 24 squares

12 button mushrooms

2 cups Chimichurri Sauce (page 140) or store-bought chimichurri sauce, divided

1. In a medium saucepan, bring 4 cups of water to a boil. Fill a large bowl with the remaining 4 cups water and 4 cups of ice for blanching the broccoli and cauliflower.
2. Add the broccoli to the boiling water. Cook for about 2 minutes, until it turns bright green. Using tongs or a hand strainer, quickly remove the broccoli from the pot and immediately plunge into the ice water. Once chilled, remove it from the ice bath.
3. Add the remaining 4 cups of ice to the bowl of water.
4. Add the cauliflower to the boiling water. Cook for 2 to 3 minutes, until softened. Using tongs or a hand strainer, quickly remove the cauliflower from the pot and immediately plunge into the ice water. Once chilled, remove it from the ice bath.
5. Place the onions, bell peppers, tofu, mushrooms, and blanched broccoli and cauliflower in a large bowl. Add 1½ cups of chimichurri and gently toss together. Cover the bowl and marinate for at least 30 minutes.
6. Preheat a grill to high heat (see Pro Tip).
7. Thread the veggies and tofu onto 12 wooden or metal skewers in this order: onion, bell pepper, tofu, broccoli, mushroom, onion, tofu, and cauliflower.
8. Grill the skewers for 3 to 4 minutes per side, until nicely charred.
9. Stack the skewers on a platter; drizzle with the remaining of chimichurri.

Per serving (3 skewers): Calories: 284; Total Fat: 19g; Saturated Fat: 3g; Trans Fat: 0g; Total Carbs: 18g; Fiber: 6g; Protein: 14g; Sodium: 200mg; Sugars: 8g

Pro Tip: *Don't have a grill? Broil the skewers in a conventional oven. Place the skewers on the middle rack and broil for 4 to 6 minutes, turning halfway through the cooking time.*

Broccoli with Butternut Squash Cheese Sauce

SERVES 4

PREP TIME: 15 minutes

COOK TIME: 10 minutes

When I was a kid, the only way my mom could get me to eat broccoli was to put it under a thick layer of cheese. I love broccoli on its own now, but I'll never turn down a ladle of vegan cheese sauce to top my steamed florets. For this healthy version of the harvesttime favorite, we blanket the steamed broccoli with an oil-free squash-based cheese sauce. It's one of the tastiest ways to pile veggies onto veggies!

30 MINUTES OR LESS, GLUTEN-FREE, OIL-FREE, ONE POT, SOY-FREE

6 cups broccoli florets

2 cups Butternut Squash Cheese Sauce (page 124), heated

1. Put 1 inch of water in a large pot and place a steamer basket in the pot. Bring the water to a boil, making sure the basket doesn't touch the water.
2. Add the broccoli to the basket and steam for 5 to 7 minutes, until tender. Transfer to a large platter and drizzle with the cheese sauce. Serve at once.

Pro Tip: *Love broccoli* and *kale? Try broccolini, which is a cross between broccoli and kale. Love cauliflower, too? Try broccoflower, a cross between broccoli and cauliflower.*

Per serving: Calories: 114; Total Fat: 4g; Saturated Fat: 1g; Trans Fat: 0g; Total Carbs: 4g; Fiber: 5g; Protein: 7g; Sodium: 78mg; Sugars: 3g

SERVES 4

PREP TIME:
10 minutes

COOK TIME:
1 hour

Oven Home Fries

Potatoes, first cultivated by the indigenous peoples of present-day Peru and Bolivia, were introduced to Europeans in the 16th century, when the Spanish explorers brought them back from the Americas. Now a staple crop the world over, potatoes are grown in about 5,000 delicious varieties. Here, we use one of my favorites, the Yukon Gold. These crisp-on-the-outside, tender-on-the-inside potatoes are an ideal pairing for any savory breakfast or entrée.

GLUTEN-FREE, NUT-FREE, SOY-FREE

1 pound Yukon Gold potatoes, cut into ¼-inch wedges

2 tablespoons olive oil

½ small onion, julienned

½ teaspoon garlic powder

½ teaspoon salt

¼ teaspoon paprika

Black pepper

1. Preheat the oven to 400°F. Line a baking sheet with parchment paper.
2. In a large bowl, combine the potatoes, olive oil, onion, garlic powder, salt, paprika, and pepper. Spread the potatoes and onion evenly on the baking sheet.
3. Roast for 40 minutes to 1 hour, stirring halfway through the cooking, until golden brown and crispy.

Pro Tip: *Red potatoes and fingerlings are a perfect swap for Yukon Gold potatoes. Just cut them the same size for even roasting.*

Per serving: Calories: 149; Total Fat: 7g; Saturated Fat: 1g; Trans Fat: 0g; Total Carbs: 19g; Fiber: 2g; Protein: 2g; Sodium: 311mg; Sugars: 2g

Pan-Sautéed Sweet Plantains

SERVES 4

PREP TIME: 5 minutes

COOK TIME: 5 minutes

Plantains are a staple food throughout tropical regions. Green plantains are starchy like potatoes and other root vegetables. Yellow plantains are sweeter and closer in texture to unripened bananas found at most supermarkets. These tender golden nuggets are wonderful as a snack or as a sweet side dish for Gallo Pinto (page 146) and Caribbean Jerk Tempeh Bowls (page 154).

30 MINUTES OR LESS, GLUTEN-FREE, NUT-FREE, ONE POT, SOY-FREE

2 tablespoons vegetable oil
1 ripe plantain
Salt

1. In a medium nonstick skillet over medium heat, heat the oil.
2. Cut off the ends of the plantain and run the tip of the knife lengthwise through the peel, making sure not to cut through the flesh. Use your hands to gently remove the peel. Cut the plantain diagonally into ½-inch slices.
3. Carefully place the plantain slices into the skillet and fry for 1 to 2 minutes per side. Transfer to a paper towel–lined plate and season with salt.

Pro Tip: *To fast-ripen plantains, roast them, unpeeled, in a 300°F oven for 40 to 45 minutes. Let cool completely in the refrigerator before using.*

Per serving: Calories: 146; Total Fat: 9g; Saturated Fat: 1g; Trans Fat: 0g; Total Carbs: 18g; Fiber: 1g; Protein: 1g; Sodium: 292mg; Sugars: 8g

SERVES 4

PREP TIME:
10 minutes, plus 20 minutes to marinate

COOK TIME:
6 minutes

Tempeh Bacon

Before going vegan, I was known to pile my plate high with bacon—and only bacon. I still love that smoky aroma, but I don't miss the burning feeling in my throat, pain in my chest, or stomach cramps. Thankfully, vegans can still enjoy that same smokiness, and tempeh is my go-to vehicle for that bacon fix. It's packed with protein and absorbs any flavors added to it. That's how vegans bring home the bacon!

NUT-FREE

2 tablespoons toasted sesame oil

2 tablespoons soy sauce, plus more as needed

1 tablespoon liquid smoke

1 tablespoon red wine vinegar

1 tablespoon smoked paprika

1 (8-ounce) package tempeh, cut into thin strips

Vegetable oil spray

1. In a large bowl, whisk together the sesame oil, soy sauce, liquid smoke, vinegar, and smoked paprika.
2. Place the tempeh strips on a large plate or in a medium shallow pan and evenly coat them with the marinade. Let marinate for 20 minutes, turning halfway through.
3. Heat a large nonstick skillet or griddle over medium heat and coat with the oil spray.
4. Evenly space the tempeh strips in the skillet. Cook for 2 to 3 minutes per side, until crispy on the edges and tender in the center. Remove from the heat.
5. Using a spatula or tongs, transfer the tempeh bacon to a paper towel–lined plate to drain.

Pro Tip: *If you don't have liquid smoke, double the amount of smoked paprika. For a spicy tempeh bacon, swap the smoked paprika for chipotle powder.*

Per serving: Calories: 192; Total Fat: 13g; Saturated Fat: 2g; Trans Fat: 0g; Total Carbs: 7g; Fiber: 1g; Protein: 12g; Sodium: 523mg; Sugars: 1g

Rustic Roasted Root Vegetables

SERVES 4

PREP TIME: 20 minutes

COOK TIME: 40 minutes

In my home, the aromas of roasted potatoes, beets, carrots, and onions mean one thing: Fall is here. Slow-roasting root veggies brings out their naturally sweet, earthy flavors, and rosemary adds a wonderfully piney fragrance. I love including whole unpeeled garlic cloves because they transform into a paste to squeeze atop these irresistible roasted veggies.

GLUTEN-FREE, NUT-FREE, SOY-FREE

- 1 large sweet potato, coarsely diced
- 1 large Yukon Gold or red potato, coarsely diced
- 2 medium beets, peeled and cut into ½-inch wedges
- 2 to 3 carrots, peeled and cut into ½-inch slices
- 1 large red onion, diced
- 8 garlic cloves, unpeeled
- ½ teaspoon salt, plus more as needed
- ¼ teaspoon black pepper, plus more as needed
- 1 to 2 tablespoons olive oil
- 1 large rosemary sprig

1. Preheat the oven to 400°F.
2. In a large bowl, combine the sweet potato, yellow potato, beets, carrots, onion, garlic, salt, pepper, and olive oil. Evenly spread the vegetables in a large roasting pan and place the rosemary sprig in the center.
3. Roast for 30 to 40 minutes, stirring halfway through the cooking time, until the vegetables are nicely browned and soft.

Pro Tip: *Any combination of root vegetables should work nicely for this recipe. If using firmer root veggies, like turnips, celery root, and rutabagas, add 30 minutes to the roasting time.*

Per serving: Calories: 176; Total Fat: 4g; Saturated Fat: 1g; Trans Fat: 0g; Total Carbs: 33g; Fiber: 5g; Protein: 4g; Sodium: 386mg; Sugars: 8g

SERVES 4

PREP TIME: 10 minutes

COOK TIME: 30 minutes

Spanish Rice

Also called arroz rojo *in my native South Texas, this tomato-based rice dish is a classic side for Tex-Mex fajitas. If you order vegan fajitas at most Tex-Mex restaurants, you have to skip the rice because it is typically cooked with chicken stock or butter. Here I bring you a chicken-free, butter-free version that's 100 percent authentic in flavor to enjoy with Refried Pintos (opposite) and Seared Portobello Fajitas (page 153).*

GLUTEN-FREE, NUT-FREE, ONE POT, SOY-FREE

2 tablespoons vegetable oil
2 cups long-grain white rice
½ small yellow onion, finely diced
2 garlic cloves, minced
¼ teaspoon ground cumin
1 to 2 tablespoons tomato paste
4 cups vegetable broth
Juice of ½ lime
¼ teaspoon dried oregano
¼ teaspoon salt, plus more as needed

1. In a large nonstick skillet over medium heat, heat the oil. Add the rice and sauté for about 5 minutes, stirring constantly, until evenly toasted.
2. Add the onion, garlic, and cumin. Sauté for 1 to 2 minutes, stirring constantly. Fold in the tomato paste.
3. Add the broth, lime juice, oregano, and salt. Bring to a boil, then reduce the heat to medium-low. Cover the skillet and simmer for 15 to 20 minutes, until all liquid is absorbed. Taste and season with more salt, if needed. Remove from the heat and uncover. Let rest for 5 minutes before fluffing with a fork.

Pro Tip: *Add any veggies you like to this basic recipe. I like to throw frozen peas, carrots, and corn in the simmer.*

Per serving: Calories: 426; Total Fat: 8g; Saturated Fat: 1g; Trans Fat: 0g; Total Carbs: 80g; Fiber: 3g; Protein: 7g; Sodium: 728mg; Sugars: 2g

Refried Pintos

SERVES 4

PREP TIME: 10 minutes

COOK TIME: 20 minutes

No pigs were harmed in the making of these easy refried pinto beans. Instead of lard, we caramelize onion and garlic to add complexity. These beans are perfect for serving with any Tex-Mex dish, like our Seared Portobello Fajitas (page 153), Tex-Mex Migas (page 61), or Tex-Mex Tofu Scramble (page 55).

30 MINUTES OR LESS, GLUTEN-FREE, NUT-FREE, ONE POT, SOY-FREE

1 tablespoon vegetable oil

¼ small yellow onion, diced

1 garlic clove, minced

½ teaspoon ground cumin

1 (15-ounce) can pinto beans, drained but not rinsed

¼ teaspoon dried oregano

2 tablespoons water, plus more as needed

¼ teaspoon salt

¼ teaspoon black pepper

Juice of ½ lime

1. In a medium saucepan over medium-high heat, heat the oil. Sauté the onion and garlic for 7 to 10 minutes, until they begin to caramelize. Add the cumin and sauté for 1 minute.
2. Add the beans, oregano, and water. Simmer for 5 minutes.
3. Using an immersion blender, puree the beans until creamy and smooth, adding more water, as needed, to reach the desired consistency. Stir in the salt, pepper, and lime juice.
4. Cook the beans for 2 to 3 more minutes, until heated through.

Pro Tip: *On their own, refried beans are a great protein-packed snack. Swap any other bean for the pintos. I love this recipe with red kidney beans, black beans, or Peruvian beans.*

Per serving: Calories: 127; Total Fat: 4g; Saturated Fat: 1g; Trans Fat: 0g; Total Carbs: 17g; Fiber: 5g; Protein: 5g; Sodium: 458mg; Sugars: 1g

Basil Pesto, page 133

CHAPTER NINE

Sauces and Dressings

Vinaigrette Trio
- Maple-Cinnamon Vinaigrette 126
- Red Wine Vinaigrette 126
- Agave-Chipotle Vinaigrette 127

Cashew Caesar Dressing 128

Butternut Squash Cheese Sauce 129

Salsa Fresca 130

Peanut Sauce 131

20-Minute Marinara 132

Basil Pesto 133

Texas-Style Barbecue Sauce 134

Cashew Hollandaise 135

Restaurant-Style Chunky Red Salsa 136

Balsamic Reduction 137

Mango Relish 138

Cashew Cream 139

Chimichurri Sauce 140

Aquafaba Mayo 141

Vinaigrette Trio

Vinaigrettes are a delightful way to brighten any leafy green. Our vinaigrette trio features three classic combinations to coat some of our new favorite salads. The sweet warmth of the Maple-Cinnamon Vinaigrette pairs well with Frisée and Apple Salad with Walnuts and Pomegranate (page 69). Classic Red Wine Vinaigrette stylishly dresses our sophisticated Chopped Fall Salad with Herbs (page 73) and Roasted Beet Salad with Baby Arugula and Macadamia Ricotta (page 70). Sweet, smoky Agave-Chipotle Vinaigrette adds a welcome crispness to the classic Tex-Mex Taco Salad (page 74).

MAKES
about 1 cup each

PREP TIME:
10 minutes

Maple-Cinnamon Vinaigrette

30 MINUTES OR LESS, GLUTEN-FREE, NUT-FREE, ONE POT, SOY-FREE

3 tablespoons apple cider vinegar
3 tablespoons maple syrup
½ teaspoon ground cinnamon
½ teaspoon salt
½ cup olive oil

Per serving (¼ cup): Calories: 279; Total Fat: 27g; Saturated Fat: 4g; Trans Fat: 0g; Total Carbs: 10g; Fiber: 0g; Protein: 0g; Sodium: 293mg; Sugars: 9g

Red Wine Vinaigrette

30 MINUTES OR LESS, GLUTEN-FREE, NUT-FREE, SOY-FREE

3 tablespoons sherry vinegar
2 tablespoons maple syrup
½ small shallot, minced
1 garlic clove, minced
1 teaspoon Dijon mustard
½ teaspoon salt
¼ teaspoon black pepper
½ cup olive oil

Per serving (¼ cup): Calories: 268; Total Fat: 27g; Saturated Fat: 4g; Trans Fat: 0g; Total Carbs: 7g; Fiber: 0g; Protein: 0g; Sodium: 322mg; Sugars: 6g

Agave-Chipotle Vinaigrette

30 MINUTES OR LESS, GLUTEN-FREE, NUT-FREE, SOY-FREE

3 tablespoons apple cider vinegar
3 tablespoons agave nectar
2 tablespoons chipotle sauce
1 garlic clove, minced
½ teaspoon dried oregano
¼ teaspoon salt, plus more as needed
⅛ teaspoon black pepper
½ cup vegetable oil

1. To make each vinaigrette, in a medium bowl, whisk together all the ingredients except the oil.
2. While whisking, slowly add the oil until emulsified.

Storing Tip: *I like storing vinaigrettes in a blender ball shaker bottle. Before serving, shake the bottle a few times for a well-combined dressing.*

Per serving (¼ cup): Calories: 290; Total Fat: 27g; Saturated Fat: 2g; Trans Fat: 0g; Total Carbs: 13g; Fiber: 0g; Protein: 0g; Sodium: 153mg; Sugars: 12g

MAKES
about 2 cups

PREP TIME:
5 minutes, plus
4 hours to soak

Cashew Caesar Dressing

This creamy fish-free spin on classic Caesar dressing is a real showstopper. Nutritional yeast adds a cheesy flavor, dulse seaweed gives a subtle seafood taste, and capers bring that anchovy-like brininess to the dressing. We use this mouthwateringly creamy dressing for Caesar Salad with Italian-Herbed Roasted Chickpeas (page 75), but I invite you to explore its versatility by letting it step in for other creamy sauces in this cookbook. Hint: Try it in the Crispy Cauliflower Po' Boys (page 100).

GLUTEN-FREE, OIL-FREE, ONE POT, SOY-FREE

1 cup raw unsalted cashews, soaked in warm water for 4 hours, drained, and rinsed

1 garlic clove, peeled

2 teaspoons Dijon mustard

1 teaspoon nutritional yeast

½ teaspoon salt

¼ teaspoon dulse seaweed flakes

Juice of ½ lemon

¾ cup cold water

2 tablespoons drained capers

1. In a blender, combine the cashews, garlic, mustard, nutritional yeast, salt, dulse, lemon juice, and water. Blend on high speed for about 2 minutes, until creamy and smooth, scraping down the sides as needed.
2. Add the capers and blend for 5 to 10 seconds. Chill the dressing before use.

Pro Tip: *Dulse seaweed flakes are typically found in the international foods section of the grocery store, near the soy sauces and rice paper. If you can't find dulse flakes, use nori (the seaweed typically used for sushi). Simply tear off a quarter sheet and add it in place of the dulse.*

Per serving (½ cup): Calories: 187; Total Fat: 14g; Saturated Fat: 3g; Trans Fat: 0g; Total Carbs: 11g; Fiber: 1g; Protein: 6g; Sodium: 483mg; Sugars: 2g

Butternut Squash Cheese Sauce

MAKES
4 cups

PREP TIME:
10 minutes, plus 20 minutes to soak

COOK TIME:
30 minutes

Boasting an abundance of vitamins, minerals, fiber, and powerful antioxidants, our silky winter squash–based cheese sauce is as nutritious as it is delicious. This oil-free sauce is seasoned to cheesy perfection and is the undisputed star of our Butternut Squash Mac and Cheese (page 152). This is a wonderful way to get even more veggies into our diets, and I use it as a topper for Broccoli with Butternut Squash Cheese Sauce (page 117) and Loaded English Jacket Potatoes (page 161).

GLUTEN-FREE, OIL-FREE, SOY-FREE

½ cup raw unsalted cashews

1 small butternut squash, peeled, seeded, and diced

1 teaspoon onion powder

1 teaspoon garlic powder

½ teaspoon ground cumin

3 to 4 tablespoons nutritional yeast

2 teaspoons Dijon mustard

1 teaspoon apple cider vinegar

1. In a small bowl, cover the cashews with hot water. Soak for 20 minutes. Drain and rinse.
2. Meanwhile, place the butternut squash in a large pot, cover with water, and bring to a boil. Cook for 20 minutes, until tender. Drain, reserving 2 cups of the cooking water.
3. In a large blender, combine the squash, cashews, onion powder, garlic powder, cumin, nutritional yeast, mustard, vinegar, and about 1 cup of the reserved liquid. Blend on high speed for 2 to 3 minutes, until the sauce is creamy and smooth, adding more liquid as needed.
4. Return the sauce to the pot and heat through.

Pro Tip: *Use this sauce as the base for a Tex-Mex queso dip. Add 1 (15-ounce) can of diced tomatoes with green chiles (drained) and heat through. Serve with corn chips.*

Per serving (1 cup): Calories: 135; Total Fat: 7g; Saturated Fat: 1g; Trans Fat: 0g; Total Carbs: 13g; Fiber: 3g; Protein: 6g; Sodium: 66mg; Sugars: 2g

MAKES
about 2 cups

PREP TIME:
15 minutes

Salsa Fresca

Also known as pico de gallo, *salsa fresca is a raw salsa made with just a few simple ingredients. It's the perfect topper for tacos, burritos, nachos, and more!*

30 MINUTES OR LESS, GLUTEN-FREE, NUT-FREE, OIL-FREE, ONE POT, SOY-FREE

2 ripe Roma (plum) tomatoes, diced
½ small onion, diced
½ jalapeño pepper, seeded and diced
1 tablespoon chopped fresh cilantro
Juice of ½ lime
¼ teaspoon salt

In a medium bowl, gently stir together the tomatoes, onion, pepper, cilantro, lime juice, and salt. Serve fresh or chilled.

Pro Tip: *Good tomatoes are key to making the perfect salsa fresca. The best tomatoes are fragrant, are free of bruises and blemishes, and have a bright red hue.*

Per serving (½ cup): Calories: 28; Total Fat: 0g; Saturated Fat: 0g; Trans Fat: 0g; Total Carbs: 5g; Fiber: 2g; Protein: 1g; Sodium: 151mg; Sugars: 3g

Peanut Sauce

MAKES
1 cup

PREP TIME:
10 minutes

Add a side of this Thai-inspired sauce to any tray of crudités, and the veggies will be gone in minutes! Seriously, this sauce is so addictive that you'll be looking for any scrap of carrot or lettuce to scoop up every bit. We use it to dress Napa Cabbage Salad (page 72) and serve it alongside Tofu Summer Rolls (page 113). This recipe calls for tamari, so our gluten-free friends can enjoy it, too, but any soy sauce works.

30 MINUTES OR LESS, GLUTEN-FREE, ONE POT

½ cup unsweetened creamy natural peanut butter
1 garlic clove, minced
2 tablespoons tamari
2 tablespoons agave nectar
1 tablespoon rice vinegar
1 tablespoon chili paste
1 teaspoon ground ginger
3 tablespoons warm water, plus more as needed

1. In a large bowl, whisk together the peanut butter, garlic, tamari, agave, vinegar, chili paste, and ginger until well combined.
2. Little by little, while whisking, add the warm water to achieve a creamy, pourable consistency.

Pro Tip: *Need a peanut-free version of this sauce? Substitute natural sunflower butter or almond butter in its place. Just make sure to get the unsweetened variety.*

Per serving (¼ cup): Calories: 240; Total Fat: 17g; Saturated Fat: 3g; Trans Fat: 0g; Total Carbs: 17g; Fiber: 2g; Protein: 9g; Sodium: 698mg; Sugars: 12g

MAKES
4 cups

PREP TIME:
5 minutes

COOK TIME:
15 minutes

20-Minute Marinara

My obsession with Italian food started when I was a kid. One summer evening my neighbor Chuck invited me for spaghetti. At that first taste of yummy marinara, I was hooked. I developed this sauce for one sole purpose: to be made in the same amount of time it takes to boil the water and to cook, drain, and plate the pasta. Mission accomplished! And it's just as flavorful as the 1-hour version I spent years making for friends and family.

30 MINUTES OR LESS, GLUTEN-FREE, NUT-FREE, ONE POT, SOY-FREE

1 tablespoon olive oil

½ small yellow onion, finely diced

1 to 2 garlic cloves, minced

1 (28-ounce) can crushed tomatoes (preferably San Marzano)

1 tablespoon tomato paste

2 teaspoons agave nectar

¼ cup fresh basil, stemmed and chopped

¼ teaspoon dried oregano

Pinch salt, plus more as needed

Pinch black pepper, plus more as needed

¼ cup water

1. Heat a medium saucepan over medium-high heat. Sauté the olive oil, onion, and garlic for 2 to 3 minutes, until the onion is translucent.
2. Stir in the tomatoes, tomato paste, agave, basil, oregano, salt, pepper, and water. Simmer, uncovered, for 15 minutes. Taste and season with more salt and pepper, if needed.

Pro Tip: *The secret to this quick and easy marinara is to use San Marzano crushed plum tomatoes and fresh basil to pull the flavors together fast.*

Per serving (1 cup): Calories: 113; Total Fat: 4g; Saturated Fat: 1g; Trans Fat: 0g; Total Carbs: 19g; Fiber: 4g; Protein: 4g; Sodium: 333mg; Sugars: 12g

Basil Pesto

MAKES
about 1 cup

PREP TIME:
10 minutes

Fresh basil shines in this tasty summery pesto. We spread this sauce on Grilled Vegetable Panini (page 97) and drizzle it over Cashew Mozzarella and Marinara Dip (page 112) and Pasta Bolognese (page 145). Add this fragrant sauce to any dish you want to perk up.

30 MINUTES OR LESS, GLUTEN-FREE, ONE POT, SOY-FREE

2 cups tightly packed fresh basil, stemmed

½ cup pine nuts, toasted

2 garlic cloves, quartered

1 teaspoon nutritional yeast

¼ teaspoon coarse sea salt

Juice of ½ lemon

¼ cup olive oil

1. In a food processor, combine the basil, pine nuts, garlic, nutritional yeast, salt, and lemon juice. Process until well combined.
2. With the processor running, slowly add the olive oil until a thick paste forms.

Pro Tip: *Refrigerate in a sealed container for up to 5 days. For a nut-free version, swap raw pumpkin seeds for the pine nuts.*

Per serving (½ cup): Calories: 273; Total Fat: 23g; Saturated Fat: 3g; Trans Fat: 0g; Total Carbs: 15g; Fiber: 3g; Protein: 5g; Sodium: 104mg; Sugars: 1g

MAKES
about 4 cups

PREP TIME:
15 minutes

COOK TIME:
15 minutes

Texas-Style Barbecue Sauce

You'll love this sauce for its rich, smoky flavor. Use it to give any veggie or sandwich a barbecue twist. We use this mildly spicy sauce for pulled pork-style Jackfruit Barbecue Sandwiches (page 99) and to glaze Baked Barbecue Cauliflower Wings (page 115). I also love substituting it for ketchup on our All-American Black Bean Burgers (page 92). Use this sauce to give any veggie or sandwich a barbecue twist.

30 MINUTES OR LESS, NUT-FREE, ONE POT

- 1 tablespoon vegetable oil
- 1 small yellow onion, diced
- 2 garlic cloves, minced
- 1 (15-ounce) can diced tomatoes with juice
- ½ cup ketchup
- ¼ cup dark molasses
- 3 tablespoons apple cider vinegar
- 1 tablespoon vegan Worcestershire sauce or steak sauce
- 1 tablespoon yellow mustard, or more as needed
- 1 tablespoon chipotle powder
- 1 teaspoon liquid smoke
- ½ teaspoon black pepper, or more as needed
- ¼ teaspoon salt, or more as needed

1. In a medium saucepan over medium-high heat, heat the oil. Add the onion and garlic. Sauté for 4 to 5 minutes, until the onion is translucent.
2. Stir in the tomatoes, ketchup, molasses, vinegar, Worcestershire, mustard, chipotle, liquid smoke, black pepper, and salt and bring to a simmer. Remove from the heat and use an immersion blender to blend until smooth. (Alternatively, let the sauce cool for 5 to 10 minutes, then transfer to a conventional blender to puree, then return to the pot.) Heat the sauce through before serving.

Pro Tip: *Chipotle powder gives this mildly spicy sauce its kick. To reduce the heat without losing any of the smokiness, swap smoked paprika for the chipotle.*

Per serving (1 cup): Calories: 157; Total Fat: 4g; Saturated Fat: 0g; Trans Fat: 0g; Total Carbs: 32g; Fiber: 2g; Protein: 2g; Sodium: 678mg; Sugars: 23g

Cashew Hollandaise

MAKES
2 cups

PREP TIME:
15 minutes, plus
20 minutes to soak

COOK TIME:
10 minutes

This is the real star of the show in our brunchtime favorite Tofu Eggs Benedict with Tempeh Bacon, Wilted Spinach, and Cashew Hollandaise (page 62). Traditionally made with cholesterol-laden eggs, our version features black Himalayan salt, which brings that eggy flavor to the table. This creamy sauce complements almost any veggie.

GLUTEN-FREE

1 cup raw unsalted cashews, soaked in hot water for 20 minutes, drained, and rinsed

2 tablespoons vegan butter or margarine

1 tablespoon nutritional yeast

½ teaspoon apple cider vinegar

½ teaspoon ground turmeric

½ teaspoon salt

¼ teaspoon black Himalayan salt

⅛ teaspoon white pepper

1 cup water, plus more as needed

In a high-speed blender, combine the cashews, butter, nutritional yeast, vinegar, turmeric, regular salt, Himalayan salt, white pepper, and water. Blend on high speed until smooth. Transfer to a saucepan over medium heat and warm before serving, adding more water as needed.

Pro Tip: *Black Himalayan salt—also known as* kala namak—*can be purchased online and at many Asian markets.*

Per serving (½ cup): Calories: 372; Total Fat: 31g; Saturated Fat: 8g; Trans Fat: 0g; Total Carbs: 18g; Fiber: 2g; Protein: 11g; Sodium: 494mg; Sugars: 3g

MAKES
about 2 cups

PREP TIME:
15 minutes

COOK TIME:
20 minutes

Restaurant-Style Chunky Red Salsa

Craving authentic salsa? It doesn't get any easier than this! For this hack version of my original chunky red salsa recipe, we skip the mortar and pestle and go for ripe-and-ready canned diced tomatoes. This quick salsa is a great snack with corn chips, or as a garnish for Seitan Chorizo Tacos *(page 149)* *and Seared Portobello Fajitas* *(page 153)**.*

GLUTEN-FREE, NUT-FREE, ONE POT, SOY-FREE

1 tablespoon vegetable oil

¼ small yellow onion, minced

1 garlic clove, minced

½ teaspoon salt, plus more as needed

¼ teaspoon ground cumin

1 small jalapeño pepper, seeded and finely diced

1 (15-ounce) can diced tomatoes with juice

1 tablespoon chipotle sauce

¼ teaspoon black pepper

Juice of 1 small lime

1 tablespoon chopped fresh cilantro

1. In a large skillet over medium-high heat, heat the oil. Add the onion, garlic, and salt. Sauté for 3 to 5 minutes, until the onion is translucent.
2. Add the cumin and jalapeño. Sauté for 2 to 3 minutes.
3. Stir in the tomatoes and their juice, chipotle sauce, and pepper. Cover the skillet and simmer for 10 minutes.
4. Stir in the lime juice and cilantro. Remove from the heat. Serve salsa warm or cold.

Pro Tip: *This is a medium-hot salsa. To increase the heat, add another jalapeño. To reduce the heat, omit or reduce the amount of chipotle sauce.*

Per serving (½ cup): Calories: 60; Total Fat: 4g; Saturated Fat: 0g; Trans Fat: 0g; Total Carbs: 7g; Fiber: 2g; Protein: 1g; Sodium: 506mg; Sugars: 4g

Balsamic Reduction

MAKES
1 cup

PREP TIME:
5 minutes

COOK TIME:
15 minutes

This two-ingredient dressing is so easy to make that you'll never buy bottled again! In just minutes, balsamic vinegar reduces to a perfectly sweet, sour glaze that can be drizzled over a variety of salads, small plates, and even desserts.

30 MINUTES OR LESS, GLUTEN-FREE, NUT-FREE, OIL-FREE, ONE POT, SOY-FREE

2 cups balsamic vinegar

2 tablespoons sugar

In a saucepan over medium heat, whisk together the vinegar and sugar. Heat until bubbling. Reduce the heat and simmer for about 15 minutes, until reduced by half, stirring occasionally. Remove from the heat and let cool completely before transferring to a squeeze bottle. Store at room temperature for up to 7 days or refrigerate up to 3 months.

Pro Tip: *Any balsamic vinegar works for this recipe. I like to use a good-quality classic balsamic from the Modena or Reggio Emilia region of Italy.*

Per serving (¼ cup): Calories: 120; Total Fat: 0g; Saturated Fat: 0g; Trans Fat: 0g; Total Carbs: 24g; Fiber: 0g; Protein: 1g; Sodium: 29mg; Sugars: 21g

MAKES
2 cups

PREP TIME:
20 minutes, plus
1 hour to chill

Mango Relish

This sweet and savory relish is the perfect topper for any tropical dish. It gives our Caribbean Island Burgers (page 98) a fruity finish and our big and bountiful Caribbean Jerk Tempeh Bowls (page 154) a colorful splash. I love using mangos throughout the year because you can always find one of the many varieties at the farmers' market—from peachy Kent mangos to citrusy Keitt mangos to tart and sweet Tommy Atkins mangos.

GLUTEN-FREE, NUT-FREE, OIL-FREE, ONE POT, SOY-FREE

2 large or 4 small mangos, finely diced

½ red bell pepper, minced

2 tablespoons chopped fresh cilantro

Juice of ½ lime

¼ teaspoon salt

In a large bowl, mix the mangos, pepper, cilantro, lime juice, and salt. Cover and refrigerate for at least 1 hour. The relish will keep well in the refrigerator for 3 to 4 days.

Pro Tip: *Give this relish some heat by swapping a spicy pepper like jalapeño or Fresno for the bell pepper.*

Per serving (½ cup): Calories: 157; Total Fat: 1g; Saturated Fat: 0g; Trans Fat: 0g; Total Carbs: 39g; Fiber: 4g; Protein: 2g; Sodium: 148mg; Sugars: 35g

Cashew Cream

MAKES
2 cups

PREP TIME:
20 minutes

Brighten any dish, like Tex-Mex Taco Salad (page 74) or Easy Three-Bean Chili (page 86), with this quick and easy nut-based cream sauce. This versatile cream sauce can serve as a delicious base for other creamy sauces and dressings. I give it a tropical makeover in my Caribbean Jerk Tempeh Bowls (page 154), turning it into a curried cashew cream.

30 MINUTES OR LESS, GLUTEN-FREE, OIL-FREE, SOY-FREE

1 cup raw unsalted cashew pieces

½ cup water, plus more for cooking cashews

Juice of 2 limes

½ teaspoon salt

1. Place the cashews in a microwave-safe bowl and add enough water to cover. Microwave on high power for 6 to 8 minutes, then let soak for 10 minutes. Drain and rinse the cashews with cold water.
2. In a high-speed blender, combine the cashews, ½ cup water, lime juice, and salt. Blend on high speed for 2 to 3 minutes, until you have a very creamy consistency, scraping down the sides of the blender with a rubber spatula halfway through.

Pro Tip: *Refrigerate in a sealed container for up to 7 days. I store this cream sauce in a squeeze bottle to decoratively drizzle over dishes.*

Per serving (½ cup): Calories: 185; Total Fat: 14g; Saturated Fat: 3g; Trans Fat: 0g; Total Carbs: 12g; Fiber: 1g; Protein: 6g; Sodium: 296mg; Sugars: 2g

MAKES
2 cups

PREP TIME:
10 minutes, plus
1 hour to chill

Chimichurri Sauce

A staple condiment and marinade for grilled meats in Argentina and Uruguay, this tangy, garlicky herbed green sauce is quickly becoming a mainstay around the world. The word chimichurri *is believed to have derived from the Basque word* tximitxurri, *which loosely means "hodge-podge" or "mix of several things in no particular order." Pair this sauce with anything grilled, like Argentinian-style Portobello Steak and Chimichurri Sandwiches (page 95) and Grilled Tofu and Veggie Kabobs (page 116).*

GLUTEN-FREE, NUT-FREE, ONE POT, SOY-FREE

3 garlic cloves, minced

1 shallot, minced

1 bunch Italian flat-leaf parsley, stems removed, leaves finely chopped

1 teaspoon fresh oregano leaves, finely chopped

¼ teaspoon red pepper flakes

1 tablespoon red wine vinegar

¼ teaspoon salt, plus more as needed

¼ teaspoon black pepper, plus more as needed

¼ cup olive oil

1. In a large bowl, combine the garlic, shallot, parsley, oregano, red pepper flakes, vinegar, salt, and pepper.
2. Little by little, add the olive oil and whisk with a fork. Taste and season with salt and pepper, as needed. Refrigerate for at least 1 hour before serving.

Storing Tip: *Keep refrigerated in a sealed container for up to 1 week.*

Per serving (½ cup): Calories: 136; Total Fat: 14g; Saturated Fat: 2g; Trans Fat: 0g; Total Carbs: 3g; Fiber: 1g; Protein: 1g; Sodium: 163mg; Sugars: 1g

Aquafaba Mayo

MAKES
2 cups

PREP TIME:
10 minutes

Aquafaba, the leftover water from cooking chickpeas, is one of the greatest culinary discoveries in modern history. This magical liquid egg replacer can star in many different foods, including meringue, macarons, and dressings. For this recipe, we use aquafaba to make a cholesterol-free mayonnaise. It's perfect to dress All-American Black Bean Burgers (page 92) and Tempeh BLTs (page 103) and to use as a base for rémoulade sauce for New Orleans-style Crispy Cauliflower Po' Boys (page 100).

30 MINUTES OR LESS, GLUTEN-FREE, NUT-FREE, ONE POT, SOY-FREE

¼ cup aquafaba (from home-cooked or canned chickpeas)

1 teaspoon salt

1 teaspoon agave nectar

¼ teaspoon cream of tartar

Juice of 1 large lime

1½ to 2 cups vegetable oil

1. In a tall jar, using an immersion blender, or in a medium bowl, using a hand mixer with the whisk attachment, whip the aquafaba for 3 to 5 minutes, until foamy.
2. Add the salt, agave, cream of tartar, and lime juice. Blend for 2 to 3 minutes.
3. While blending, slowly add the oil as the mayo begins to thicken (see Pro Tip). Transfer to a sealable container and chill until ready to use.

Pro Tip: *The total amount of oil needed depends on the aquafaba's viscosity. Thicker aquafaba (like what you usually get from Kroger brand chickpeas) requires about 1½ cups oil. Other brands can have thinner aquafaba, so add more oil to get your desired mayo-like consistency.*

Per serving (2 tablespoons): Calories: 214; Total Fat: 24g; Saturated Fat: 2g; Trans Fat: 0g; Total Carbs: 1g; Fiber: 0g; Protein: 0g; Sodium: 6mg; Sugars: 0g

Butternut Squash Mac and Cheese, page 152

CHAPTER TEN

Entrées

Southwestern Black Bean and Quinoa Bowls 144

Pasta Bolognese 145

Gallo Pinto (Central American Rice and Beans) 146

Portobello-Pineapple Poke Bowls 147

Sweet Potato and Shiitake Mushroom Risotto 148

Seitan Chorizo Tacos 149

Wild Rice and Lentil Stuffed Acorn Squash 150

Tofu Chops with Caramelized Apple and Onion 151

Butternut Squash Mac and Cheese 152

Seared Portobello Fajitas 153

Caribbean Jerk Tempeh Bowls 154

Wild Mushroom and Vegetable Fried Rice 155

Easy Chana Masala 156

Macadamia-Cashew Carbonara with Tempeh Bacon 157

Herbed Oyster Mushroom White Cream Flatbread 158

Seitan Sausage Jambalaya 159

Mushroom-Lentil Shepherd's Pie 160

Loaded English Jacket Potatoes 161

Spicy Bean Tamales 162

Spanish Chorizo and Vegetable Paella 164

SERVES 4

PREP TIME: 15 minutes

COOK TIME: 15 minutes

Southwestern Black Bean and Quinoa Bowls

This Santa Fe–style bowl is simple and satisfying. When I first went vegan, it was a go-to meal. In fact, it remains a favorite. I love making this protein-packed meal at the end of an active day.

30 MINUTES OR LESS, GLUTEN-FREE, ONE POT, SOY-FREE

- 2 teaspoons vegetable oil, divided
- 1 cup frozen corn kernels, thawed
- ½ teaspoon salt, divided, plus more as needed
- 2 cups canned black beans, drained and rinsed
- ½ teaspoon garlic powder
- ½ teaspoon onion powder
- ½ teaspoon dark chili powder
- 2 cups cooked quinoa (from 1 cup uncooked)
- 1 Hass avocado, cut into 8 wedges
- 2 radishes, trimmed and thinly sliced
- ½ cup pumpkin seeds, toasted
- ½ cup Salsa Fresca (page 130) or store-bought fresh red salsa
- ¼ cup Cashew Cream (page 139)
- ¼ cup fresh cilantro leaves, chopped
- 1 lime, quartered

1. In a large nonstick skillet over medium-high heat, heat 1 teaspoon of the oil. Add the corn and ¼ teaspoon of the salt. Sauté for 7 to 10 minutes, stirring occasionally, or until the corn is nicely browned. Transfer to a plate.
2. In the same skillet, stir together the remaining 1 teaspoon of oil, the beans, garlic powder, onion powder, chili powder, and the remaining ¼ teaspoon of salt.
3. Fold in the quinoa and cook for about 5 minutes, until heated through, stirring occasionally. Remove from the heat, taste, and adjust the seasoning, if needed.
4. Evenly mound the bean and quinoa mix in the center of the serving bowls. Around it place the toasted corn, avocado, radish slices, pumpkin seeds, and salsa.
5. Drizzle with the cashew cream and sprinkle with the cilantro. Serve each bowl with a lime quarter.

Per serving: Calories: 646; Total Fat: 26g; Saturated Fat: 4g; Trans Fat: 0g; Total Carbs: 81g; Fiber: 16g; Protein: 24g; Sodium: 600mg; Sugars: 3g

Pasta Bolognese

SERVES 4

PREP TIME: 15 minutes

COOK TIME: 25 minutes

Seitan-based Italian sausage and marinara come together to create this rich, meaty homestyle favorite. Make this for any meat lover, and I assure you the person will ask for seconds! Pair this perfect pasta bowl with a nice Chianti, Barolo, or cabernet sauvignon for an extra-special night.

2 tablespoons olive oil, divided

2 links Italian Sausage (page 108) or store-bought plant-based Italian sausage, crumbled

1 garlic clove, minced

½ small yellow onion, finely diced

1 small carrot, finely diced

1 celery stalk, finely diced

2 cups 20-Minute Marinara (page 132) or store-bought marinara

1 pound rigatoni pasta

¼ cup Basil Pesto (page 133) or store-bought vegan pesto

2 tablespoons grated vegan Parmesan cheese

1. Heat a medium saucepan over medium-high heat. Add 1 tablespoon of the olive oil and the sausage. Sauté for 5 to 7 minutes, until nicely browned. Transfer the sausage to a bowl and set aside.
2. In the same saucepan, combine the remaining 1 tablespoon of oil, the garlic, onion, carrot, and celery. Sauté for 5 to 7 minutes, until tender. Stir in the sautéed sausage and the marinara. Reduce the heat to medium-low, cover the pan, and let simmer while you cook the pasta.
3. Bring a large pot of water to a boil. Add the rigatoni and cook for 10 to 12 minutes, stirring occasionally, until al dente. Drain the pasta and return it to the pot.
4. Transfer the Bolognese sauce to the large pot and combine with the pasta. Serve hot, garnished with the pesto and cheese.

Pro Tip: *Use a food processor to crumble the sausages. And try any other sausages from Seitan Sausage 3 Ways (page 106). For a spicier dish, I recommend the Apple-Sage Andouille Sausage.*

Per serving: Calories: 407; Total Fat: 12g; Saturated Fat: 2g; Trans Fat: 0g; Total Carbs: 50g; Fiber: 6g; Protein: 30g; Sodium: 700mg; Sugars: 9g

SERVES 4

PREP TIME: 15 minutes

COOK TIME: 20 minutes

Gallo Pinto (Central American Rice and Beans)

Costa Rica claims this Afro-Caribbean dish originated in the 1930s, in the town of San Jose. Nicaragua claims it originated on its Caribbean coast long before that time. In an effort to officially claim the dish as their own, both countries took to battle in the Guinness Book of World Records. *Costa Rica won in 2003 by cooking 965 pounds of gallo pinto in one pot. Two weeks later, Nicaragua made 1,200 pounds. Nicaragua claimed the most recent title on September 15, 2007—known as Gallo Pinto Day.*

GLUTEN-FREE, NUT-FREE, ONE POT, SOY-FREE

- 1 tablespoon vegetable oil
- ½ cup diced yellow or white onion
- ½ cup diced green bell pepper
- 2 (15-ounce) cans red beans, undrained
- 3 cups day-old steamed white rice (from 1 cup uncooked)
- Salt and black pepper
- 1 Hass avocado, sliced into wedges
- Pan-Sautéed Sweet Plantains (page 119)

1. In a large nonstick skillet over medium-high heat, heat the oil. Sauté the onion and bell pepper for 1 to 2 minutes.
2. Stir in the beans and their liquid. Simmer for 7 to 10 minutes, until most of the liquid has evaporated.
3. Add the rice and blend well. Sauté for 3 to 5 minutes, stirring occasionally. Taste and season with salt and pepper. Serve with avocado wedges and plantains.

Did you know? *Many variations of this Afro-Caribbean mainstay exist throughout Latin America and the Caribbean. In El Salvador and Honduras, it's called* casamiento, *which means "marriage." In Cuba, it's called* Moros y Cristianos, *translating to "Moors and Christians."*

Per serving: Calories: 540; Total Fat: 19g; Saturated Fat: 2g; Trans Fat: 0g; Total Carbs: 81g; Fiber: 16g; Protein: 16g; Sodium: 909mg; Sugars: 10g

Portobello-Pineapple Poke Bowls

SERVES 4

PREP TIME: 20 minutes, plus 20 minutes to marinate

COOK TIME: 10 minutes

Cubes of grilled marinated portobello steaks are served alongside brown rice, avocado, crisp veggies, and grilled pineapple in this unique poke bowl.

GLUTEN-FREE, NUT-FREE

¼ cup Aquafaba Mayo (page 141) or store-bought vegan mayo

1 teaspoon sriracha hot sauce

1 tablespoon toasted sesame oil

¼ cup tamari

2 tablespoons agave nectar

1 tablespoon rice vinegar

2 garlic cloves, minced

1 tablespoon minced peeled fresh ginger

1 tablespoon red pepper flakes

4 portobello mushrooms, stems and gills removed

4 (¼-inch-thick) ring slices of fresh pineapple

2 cups cooked brown rice (from about 1 cup uncooked)

4 cups mixed baby greens

2 large carrots, thinly sliced on a diagonal

1 large English cucumber, unpeeled, thinly sliced on a diagonal

1 cup shelled fresh edamame

2 Hass avocados, each cut into 8 wedges

4 scallions, green parts only, diced

1. In a small bowl, whisk together the mayo and sriracha. Refrigerate while you prepare the rest of the recipe.
2. In another small bowl, whisk together the sesame oil, tamari, agave, vinegar, garlic, ginger, and red pepper flakes. Place the portobello caps on a large plate or in a medium shallow pan and evenly coat them with the marinade. Let marinate for 20 minutes.
3. Preheat a grill to medium-high heat.
4. Grill the mushrooms and the pineapple slices over a direct flame for 4 to 5 minutes per side. Remove and let rest for 5 minutes. (Alternatively, in batches in a preheated cast-iron skillet over medium-high heat, fast-sear the portobello caps and pineapple slices. Use a second cast-iron skillet or grill press to press down on the mushrooms and pineapple. Cook for 3 to 4 minutes per side.)
5. Quarter the pineapple rings and cut the portobellos into ½-inch squares.
6. To assemble the bowls, place ½ cup of rice in the center of each bowl. Arrange the greens, carrots, cucumber, edamame, pineapple, and avocado over the rice. Top the rice with the grilled portobellos, sriracha, and scallion.

Per serving: Calories: 542; Total Fat: 29g; Saturated Fat: 3g; Trans Fat: 0g; Total Carbs: 65g; Fiber: 12g; Protein: 12g; Sodium: 984mg; Sugars: 26g

Pro Tip: *If using store-bought vegan mayo, I recommend JUST mayo; you can find it at most major supermarkets, including Walmart.*

SERVES 4

PREP TIME: 20 minutes

COOK TIME: 45 minutes

Sweet Potato and Shiitake Mushroom Risotto

Sweet potato adds the perfect touch of sweetness to this creamy autumn risotto. The secret to perfect risotto is constantly stirring while cooking it over low heat. This elegant rice dish pairs nicely with an earthy red wine or full-bodied white.

GLUTEN-FREE, ONE POT

2 tablespoons vegan butter or margarine

2 cups stemmed and julienned fresh shiitake mushrooms

½ small yellow onion, finely diced

2 teaspoons chopped fresh sage, divided

2 garlic cloves, minced

1 cup arborio rice

1 cup canned sweet potato puree, divided

1 cup dry white wine

2½ cups vegetable broth, divided

½ teaspoon salt, plus more as needed

1 tablespoon chopped fresh Italian flat-leaf parsley

¼ teaspoon black pepper, plus more as needed

2 tablespoons grated vegan Parmesan cheese

1. In a medium saucepan over medium heat, melt the butter. Add the mushrooms, onion, 1 teaspoon of the sage, and the garlic. Sauté for 5 to 7 minutes, until the onion is translucent. Fold in the rice. Sauté for 1 minute, stirring constantly.
2. Stir in half the pureed sweet potato, the wine, ½ cup of the broth, and the salt. Increase the heat and bring to a boil. Reduce the heat to medium-low and simmer for 5 to 7 minutes, stirring constantly, until the liquid is reduced by half.
3. Add the remaining 2 cups of broth. Cook for 25 minutes, until the rice is tender, stirring occasionally. Remove from the heat.
4. Stir in the remaining sweet potato puree, the parsley, and pepper. Taste and season with more salt and pepper, if needed. Serve hot, topped with the Parmesan and the remaining 1 teaspoon of sage.

Pro Tip: *Arborio rice is my go-to rice for risotto, but sushi rice also works.*

Per serving: Calories: 361; Total Fat: 8g; Saturated Fat: 4g; Trans Fat: 0g; Total Carbs: 56g; Fiber: 6g; Protein: 7g; Sodium: 724mg; Sugars: 6g

Seitan Chorizo Tacos

SERVES 4 (MAKES 12 TACOS)

PREP TIME: 15 minutes

COOK TIME: 10 minutes

Mexican chorizo is a highly spiced ground pork sausage made with vinegar, chiles, and a variety of herbs and spices. For this Taco Tuesday special, we turn to our seitan Spanish Chorizo and sauté it with a bold south-of-the-border spice blend.

30 MINUTES OR LESS, ONE POT

- 1 teaspoon vegetable oil
- 1 recipe Spanish Chorizo (page 106) or 4 links Tofurky kielbasa, chopped or crumbled
- 1½ teaspoons dark chili powder
- 1 teaspoon chipotle powder
- ½ teaspoon garlic powder
- ½ teaspoon dried oregano
- 1 tablespoon tomato sauce
- 1 teaspoon apple cider vinegar
- 12 corn tortillas, warmed
- ½ medium yellow onion, finely diced
- ¼ cup fresh cilantro, chopped
- ½ cup Cashew Cream (page 139)
- ½ cup Restaurant-Style Chunky Red Salsa (page 136) or store-bought red salsa
- 3 limes, quartered

1. In a skillet over medium-high heat, heat the oil. Stir in the chorizo, chili powder, chipotle powder, garlic powder, oregano, tomato sauce, and vinegar. Sauté for 5 to 7 minutes, until nicely browned.
2. Serve on warm corn tortillas with the diced onion and cilantro. Drizzle with the cashew cream and salsa. Serve with lime wedges.

Pro Tip: *For a lighter dish, substitute 1 pound diced button mushrooms for the chorizo. Swap toasted sesame oil for the vegetable oil, and use the same spice blend. Sauté for 10 to 12 minutes, stirring occasionally, until most of the liquid evaporates.*

Per serving (3 tacos): Calories: 499; Total Fat: 12g; Saturated Fat: 1g; Trans Fat: 0g; Total Carbs: 50g; Fiber: 7g; Protein: 51g; Sodium: 1,071mg; Sugars: 5g

SERVES 4

PREP TIME: 20 minutes

COOK TIME: about 1 hour

Wild Rice and Lentil Stuffed Acorn Squash

Slow-roasted, then stuffed with herbed lentils, mushrooms, wild rice, and walnuts, this acorn squash is a holiday main course that truly captures the essence of fall and is the perfect entrée for an autumn dinner party.

GLUTEN-FREE, SOY-FREE

2 acorn squash, halved and seeded
2 to 3 tablespoons olive oil, divided
2 teaspoons salt, divided
2 cups water
½ cup wild rice, brown rice, or quinoa, rinsed
½ cup finely diced yellow onion
1 garlic clove, minced
½ cup finely diced button mushrooms
1½ cups cooked lentils (from about 1 cup uncooked)
1 tablespoon herbes de Provence
2 tablespoons dry red wine
½ cup walnut pieces
¼ cup chopped fresh parsley, divided
½ teaspoon black pepper

1. Preheat the oven to 350°F.
2. Place the squash halves on a baking sheet, cut-side up. Brush the cut sides with 1 to 2 tablespoons of the olive oil. Lightly sprinkle with 1 teaspoon of the salt. Roast for 40 to 50 minutes, until tender.
3. While the squash roasts, in a medium saucepan over medium-high heat, bring the water to a boil. Reduce the heat to low and add the wild rice. Cover the pan and cook for 35 to 40 minutes, or until all the water is absorbed. Remove from the heat and fluff with a fork.
4. When the squash has about 20 minutes left to cook, in a large skillet over medium-high heat, heat the remaining 1 tablespoon of oil. Sauté the onion for 2 to 3 minutes, until translucent, stirring occasionally.
5. Add the garlic and mushrooms. Sauté for 2 to 3 minutes, stirring occasionally. Stir in the lentils, wild rice, herbes de Provence, and wine. Reduce the heat, cover the skillet, and simmer for 5 to 7 minutes. Stir in the walnuts, 2 tablespoons of the parsley, the remaining 1 teaspoon of salt, and the pepper.
6. Stuff the squash halves with the lentil and rice mixture and garnish with the remaining 2 tablespoons of parsley.

Per serving: Calories: 408; Total Fat: 19g; Saturated Fat: 2g; Trans Fat: 0g; Total Carbs: 52g; Fiber: 12g; Protein: 13g; Sodium: 1,255mg; Sugars: 3g

Pro Tip: *Any winter squash works for this dish. Butternut and delicata squashes bring added sweetness.*

Tofu Chops with Caramelized Apple and Onion

SERVES 4

PREP TIME:
15 minutes, plus 30 minutes to marinate

COOK TIME:
25 minutes

Tofu is one of my favorite plant-based proteins because of its versatility. For this dish, tofu steps in for pork in this animal-friendly take on the fall classic. To give our tofu its pork-like taste, we marinate it, then sear it in nutty sesame oil. Served alongside butter-caramelized green apple and onion, this flavorful dish never disappoints!

GLUTEN-FREE, NUT-FREE

- **1 (16-ounce) package extra-firm tofu, cut into 4 steaks**
- **2 garlic cloves, finely chopped, divided**
- **¼ cup vegetable broth**
- **½ teaspoon apple cider vinegar**
- **½ teaspoon ground sage**
- **½ teaspoon salt, plus more as needed**
- **½ teaspoon black pepper, plus more as needed**
- **1 tablespoon toasted sesame oil**
- **1 tablespoon vegan butter or margarine, divided**
- **1 medium green apple, unpeeled, cored and thinly sliced**
- **1 large yellow onion, julienned**

1. In a large bowl, combine the tofu, half the garlic, the broth, vinegar, sage, salt, and pepper. Cover and marinate at room temperature for 30 minutes, turning occasionally.
2. Heat a cast-iron skillet over medium-high heat. Add the sesame oil and sear the tofu steaks for 5 to 7 minutes per side, until well browned. Remove from the pan and set aside.
3. In the same skillet, melt the butter. Add the apple and onion. Sauté for 5 to 7 minutes, stirring occasionally, until the onion is caramelized. Stir in the remaining garlic and sauté for 2 minutes.
4. Return the tofu steaks to the skillet and cook for 2 minutes per side. Serve hot.

Pro Tip: *Toasted sesame oil is the key ingredient to giving that pork-like flavor to plant-based proteins like tempeh and tofu. Try different vegetable and nut oils for variety.*

Per serving: Calories: 206; Total Fat: 13g; Saturated Fat: 3g; Trans Fat: 0g; Total Carbs: 13g; Fiber: 2g; Protein: 12g; Sodium: 360mg; Sugars: 8g

SERVES 4

PREP TIME:
15 minutes

COOK TIME:
15 minutes

Butternut Squash Mac and Cheese

Creamy butternut squash, cashews, and nutritional yeast blend into a luscious cheese sauce for a healthy transformation of a family favorite. What was once a childhood indulgence is now a guiltless pleasure. In my home, Sunday nights are for mac and cheese, which we love to pair with a crisp sauvignon blanc. For a touch of sophistication, add a dash of truffle oil.

30 MINUTES OR LESS, ONE POT, SOY-FREE

1 pound elbow pasta

1 recipe Butternut Squash Cheese Sauce (page 129)

Dash truffle oil (optional)

Salt

1. Bring a large pot of water to a boil. Add the pasta and cook for 6 to 8 minutes, stirring occasionally, until al dente. Drain and set aside.
2. In the same pot over medium heat, combine the cheese sauce and oil (if using). Cook for 4 to 5 minutes, stirring constantly, until warmed through. Fold in the pasta. Taste and season with salt, if needed. Serve hot.

Pro Tip: *To make this dish gluten-free, use quinoa or corn-based pasta instead. These alternative pastas are difficult to overcook.*

Per serving: Calories: 335; Total Fat: 8g; Saturated Fat: 1g; Trans Fat: 0g; Total Carbs: 54g; Fiber: 5g; Protein: 13g; Sodium: 211mg; Sugars: 4g

Seared Portobello Fajitas

SERVES 4

PREP TIME: 10 minutes, plus 20 minutes to marinate

COOK TIME: 15 minutes

The original fajitas were invented by ranch workers in the 1930s living along the Texas-Mexico border. The workers were given skirt steaks (a.k.a. fajitas *in Spanish) as part of their wages, which they cooked and served on tortillas. Now fajitas are an American staple and you don't even need meat to make them!*

GLUTEN-FREE

FOR THE FAJITAS

- 2 tablespoons vegetable oil, divided
- 1 tablespoon tamari
- 1 teaspoon chipotle powder
- 1 teaspoon garlic powder
- 1 teaspoon onion powder
- ½ teaspoon ground cumin
- ¼ teaspoon black pepper, plus more as needed
- 4 large portobello mushrooms, stems and gills removed
- ½ medium yellow onion, julienned
- ½ green bell pepper, julienned
- ½ red bell pepper, julienned
- Salt
- 12 corn tortillas, warmed

FOR SERVING (OPTIONAL)

- ½ cup Restaurant-Style Chunky Red Salsa (page 136) or store-bought red salsa
- ½ cup Easy Guacamole (page 111) or store-bought guacamole
- ¼ cup Cashew Cream (page 139)
- 2 limes, quartered

1. **Make the fajitas:** In a small bowl, whisk 1 tablespoon of the oil, the tamari, chipotle powder, garlic powder, onion powder, cumin, and pepper.
2. Place the mushroom caps on a large plate or in a shallow medium pan and evenly coat them with the marinade. Let marinate for 20 minutes.
3. In a large cast-iron skillet over medium-high heat, heat the remaining 1 tablespoon of oil. In 2 batches, place the mushroom caps in the skillet and use a second cast-iron skillet or grill press to press down on the mushrooms. Cook for 3 to 4 minutes per side, until nicely browned. Return the cooked mushroom caps to the plate.
4. In the same skillet, sauté the onion and bell peppers for 4 to 5 minutes. Season with salt and pepper to taste. Remove from the heat.
5. Cut the mushrooms into ½-inch strips and place atop the onion and peppers in the skillet.
6. Serve with warm tortillas and garnishes of choice.

Per serving (3 tortillas): Calories: 216; Total Fat: 9g; Saturated Fat: 1g; Trans Fat: 0g; Total Carbs: 29g; Fiber: 4g; Protein: 6g; Sodium: 435mg; Sugars: 5g

Pro Tip: *For a real Tex-Mex experience, serve these fajitas with a side of Spanish Rice (page 122) and Refried Pintos (page 123).*

SERVES 4

PREP TIME: 15 minutes, plus 20 minutes to marinate

COOK TIME: 30 minutes

Caribbean Jerk Tempeh Bowls

A fragrant spice rub brings Jamaican flair to this dish. Served alongside fluffy white rice and a host of toppings, the drizzle of curried cashew cream adds a vibrant finish. You can use regular curry powder if you can't find the Jamaican kind.

GLUTEN-FREE

FOR THE JERK TEMPEH

1 tablespoon olive oil

1 tablespoon maple syrup

Juice of 1 lime

2 teaspoons ground allspice

1 teaspoon dried thyme

1 teaspoon salt

½ teaspoon black pepper

1 small jalapeño pepper, seeded and finely chopped

2 garlic cloves, minced

1 (8-ounce) package tempeh, cut into 4 (¼-inch) slabs

FOR THE SAUCE

⅓ cup Cashew Cream (page 139)

1½ teaspoons Jamaican curry powder (see headnote)

FOR THE BOWLS

2 cups cooked white rice (from 1 cup uncooked)

1 recipe Pan-Sautéed Sweet Plantains (page 119)

1 cup canned red kidney beans, drained and rinsed

2 Hass avocados, cubed

½ cup Mango Relish (page 138)

¼ cup unsweetened coconut flakes, toasted

1. **Make the jerk tempeh:** In a small bowl, whisk together the olive oil, maple syrup, lime juice, allspice, thyme, salt, pepper, jalapeño, and garlic. Place the tempeh slabs on a large plate or in a shallow pan and evenly coat them with the marinade. Let marinate for 20 minutes.
2. Heat a grill pan or nonstick skillet over medium-high heat. Grill the tempeh for about 5 minutes per side, until nicely charred. Remove from the heat.
3. **Make the sauce:** In a small bowl, whisk the cashew cream and curry powder. Refrigerate until ready to use.
4. **Assemble the bowls:** Place ½ cup of the cooked rice in the center of each bowl. Arrange the plantains, beans, cubed avocado, mango relish, coconut, and jerk tempeh on top. Drizzle with the cashew cream.

Pro Tip: *No tempeh? Use tofu. Cut into 4 even slabs and marinate as directed. Chargrill or sear for 7 minutes per side, or until nicely blackened.*

Per serving: Calories: 650; Total Fat: 34g; Saturated Fat: 7g; Trans Fat: 0g; Total Carbs: 74g; Fiber: 12g; Protein: 20g; Sodium: 1,121mg; Sugars: 21g

Wild Mushroom and Vegetable Fried Rice

SERVES 4

PREP TIME:
20 minutes

COOK TIME:
20 minutes

Wild mushrooms, which are fast-sautéed to bring out their deep, rich, meaty flavors, add complexity to this classic dish. Then we combine an assortment of veggies and brown rice for a healthy twist on a restaurant-style favorite.

GLUTEN-FREE, NUT-FREE, ONE POT

- 2 tablespoons vegetable oil, divided
- 1½ pounds fresh mixed wild mushrooms, sliced, divided
- 1 tablespoon toasted sesame oil
- 1 small carrot, thinly sliced into rings
- 1 small celery stalk, thinly sliced
- ½ red bell pepper, julienned
- ¼ teaspoon red pepper flakes
- 1 tablespoon grated peeled fresh ginger
- 6 scallions, green parts only, diced
- 3 cups cooked short-grain brown rice (from about 2½ cups uncooked)
- ¼ cup soy sauce
- ½ teaspoon salt, plus more as needed
- ¼ cup frozen shelled edamame
- ¼ cup frozen corn kernels

1. In a large wok or nonstick stir-fry pan over medium-high heat, heat 1 tablespoon of the vegetable oil. Add half the mushrooms. Sauté for 5 minutes, stirring constantly, or until the mushrooms are tender and golden brown. Transfer to a plate.
2. In the same wok, heat the remaining 1 tablespoon of oil. Sauté the remaining mushrooms. Transfer to the plate.
3. In the same wok, heat the sesame oil. Add the carrot, celery, red bell pepper, red pepper flakes, ginger, and three-quarters of the scallion greens. Sauté for 2 to 3 minutes, stirring occasionally, until the vegetables begin to soften.
4. Increase the heat and add the rice, soy sauce, and salt. Sauté for 2 minutes, stirring constantly. Add the edamame, corn, and cooked mushrooms. Cook for 2 to 3 minutes, stirring constantly, until the fried rice is heated through. Taste and season with more salt, if needed. Serve garnished with the remaining scallion greens.

Per serving: Calories: 350; Total Fat: 13g; Saturated Fat: 1g; Trans Fat: 0g; Total Carbs: 50g; Fiber: 8g; Protein: 12g; Sodium: 1,036mg; Sugars: 6g

Pro Tip: *The trick to making the perfect stir-fry is in the pan. If you cook with natural gas, either a wok or a stir-fry pan will work. If you cook on a flattop stove, use a stir-fry pan because the wok's rounded bottom will prevent the pan from collecting enough heat.*

SERVES 4

PREP TIME: 15 minutes

COOK TIME: 30 minutes

Easy Chana Masala

This chickpea curry is arguably the most popular naturally vegetarian dish of India. On a trip to visit my brother and sister-in-law in Galicia, Spain, during my early vegan days, my brother's British friends introduced me to it, explaining that chana masala was one of the most beloved dishes in the UK. After one bite, it was one of mine, too! This quick version always hits the spot.

GLUTEN-FREE, NUT-FREE, ONE POT, SOY-FREE

2 tablespoons vegetable oil

2 teaspoons ground cumin

½ teaspoon ground turmeric

1 small yellow onion, chopped

1 small jalapeño pepper, seeded and thinly sliced

½ teaspoon salt, plus more as needed

1 tablespoon minced peeled fresh ginger

4 garlic cloves, minced

½ cup fresh cilantro, finely chopped, divided

2 teaspoons ground coriander

1½ teaspoons garam masala

1 (28-ounce) can crushed tomatoes

2 (15-ounce) cans chickpeas, drained and rinsed

Juice of ½ lemon

1. Heat a large pot over medium heat. Add the oil, cumin, and turmeric. Toast the spices for 1 minute, stirring occasionally. Stir in the onion, jalapeño, and salt. Sauté for 5 to 6 minutes, until the onion is tender.
2. Add the ginger, garlic, and half the cilantro. Sauté for 1 minute, stirring occasionally.
3. Stir in the coriander and garam masala. Sauté for 1 minute, stirring constantly.
4. Add the crushed tomatoes and chickpeas. Increase the heat and bring to a simmer. Cook, uncovered, for 15 to 20 minutes. Remove from the heat and stir in the lemon juice. Taste and season with more salt, if needed. Serve hot, garnished with the remaining cilantro.

Fun Fact: Chana masala *literally translates to "mixed spice small chickpeas." The larger chickpeas we use in the Western world are called "chole." So, this dish should be called "Chole Masala," but since most Indian restaurants in the West interchange* chole *and* chana *for the masala, I went with the most recognizable Western name.*

Per serving: Calories: 345; Total Fat: 11g; Saturated Fat: 1g; Trans Fat: 0g; Total Carbs: 52g; Fiber: 14g; Protein: 15g; Sodium: 854mg; Sugars: 16g

Macadamia-Cashew Carbonara with Tempeh Bacon

SERVES 4

PREP TIME:
15 minutes, plus overnight to soak

COOK TIME:
20 minutes

Pure bliss is what you get from this plant-based twist on the creamy Roman original. Our succulent sauce is made with rich, buttery macadamias, cashew cream, and savory seasonings. Himalayan black salt brings a subtle eggyness, and truffle oil adds elegance—topped with smoky tempeh bacon and Parmesan for a sophisticated pasta dinner.

- **1 pound linguine**
- **1 cup raw unsalted macadamia nuts, soaked in water overnight, drained, and rinsed**
- **¼ cup nutritional yeast**
- **1 teaspoon salt, plus more as needed**
- **1 teaspoon onion powder**
- **1 teaspoon garlic powder**
- **½ teaspoon ground turmeric**
- **½ teaspoon truffle oil (optional)**
- **¼ teaspoon white pepper**
- **⅛ teaspoon Himalayan black salt**
- **2 cups water**
- **1 cup Cashew Cream (page 139)**
- **1 cup unsweetened almond milk**
- **1 recipe Tempeh Bacon (page 120)**
- **¼ cup grated vegan Parmesan cheese**
- **2 tablespoons chopped fresh parsley**

1. Bring a large pot of water to a boil. Add the pasta and cook for 10 to 12 minutes, stirring occasionally, until al dente. Drain and set aside.
2. In a high-speed blender, combine the macadamias, nutritional yeast, salt, onion powder, garlic powder, turmeric, truffle oil (if using), white pepper, black salt, water, cashew cream, and almond milk. Blend on high speed until very creamy and smooth. Transfer to the pasta pot and cook over medium heat for 4 to 5 minutes, stirring constantly, until warmed.
3. Fold in the pasta. Taste and season with more salt, if needed. Serve piping hot, garnished with the tempeh bacon, Parmesan, and parsley.

Pro Tip: *A dry, crisp white wine is the perfect accompaniment. Try a pinot grigio, Chablis, or Picpoul de Pinet.*

Per serving: Calories: 1,010; Total Fat: 52g; Saturated Fat: 8g; Trans Fat: 0g; Total Carbs: 108g; Fiber: 11g; Protein: 39g; Sodium: 1,573mg; Sugars: 6g

SERVES 4

PREP TIME: 15 minutes

COOK TIME: 20 to 25 minutes

Herbed Oyster Mushroom White Cream Flatbread

Woodsy oyster mushrooms are rubbed together with sage, rosemary, and thyme for this gourmet flatbread experience. Pair your flatbreads with a medium-bodied pinot noir or a rich, buttery chardonnay.

NUT-FREE

- 3 tablespoons vegan butter or margarine
- 2 tablespoons all-purpose flour
- 2 cups unsweetened soymilk
- 1 teaspoon nutritional yeast
- ¼ teaspoon black pepper, divided
- 1 tablespoon olive oil
- ½ teaspoon dried sage
- ½ teaspoon dried rosemary
- ½ teaspoon dried thyme
- ¼ teaspoon salt
- 8 ounces fresh oyster mushrooms, separated and torn into bite-size pieces
- 4 vegan white naan or other small flatbreads
- 1 medium shallot, julienned

1. Preheat the oven to 400°F. Line a large rimmed baking sheet or sheet pan with parchment paper.
2. Heat a medium saucepan over medium-high heat. Add the butter to melt. Little by little, add the flour, whisking constantly.
3. While whisking, add the soymilk, nutritional yeast, and ⅛ teaspoon of the pepper. Cook, whisking, for about 5 minutes, until the cream sauce thickens to gravy-like consistency. Remove from the heat.
4. In a large bowl, whisk the olive oil, sage, rosemary, thyme, salt, and the remaining ⅛ teaspoon of pepper. Add the mushrooms. Use your hands to gently massage and lightly coat the mushrooms with the spices.
5. Place the naan on the lined baking sheet. Generously spread some of the white sauce over each flatbread. Top with the shallot and herbed mushrooms. Lightly drizzle with the remaining white sauce.
6. Bake for 15 to 18 minutes, until the flatbread edges are browned and crispy.

Per serving: Calories: 458; Total Fat: 16g; Saturated Fat: 7g; Trans Fat: 0g; Total Carbs: 61g; Fiber: 6g; Protein: 17g; Sodium: 727mg; Sugars: 4g

Pro Tip: *For the perfect white sauce, use Miyoko's Creamery European Style Cultured Vegan Butter.*

Seitan Sausage Jambalaya

SERVES 4

PREP TIME:
20 minutes

COOK TIME:
45 minutes

Get transported to New Orleans' French Quarter with this plant-based twist on sausage jambalaya. For this recipe, we pan-sauté seitan-based Apple-Sage Andouille Sausage and Cajun mirepoix before slow-simmering with rice and creole seasonings. The end result is a flavor explosion! Turn on some Louis Armstrong while making this dish for a deliciously dirty New Orleans experience.

NUT-FREE, ONE POT, SOY-FREE

2 tablespoons vegetable oil

2 links Apple-Sage Andouille Sausage (page 109) or Tofurky Andouille sausage links, cut diagonally into ⅓-inch slices

2 celery stalks, finely diced

1 green bell pepper, finely diced

1 small yellow onion, finely diced

2 garlic cloves, minced

5 scallions, green and white parts, diced

2 cups long-grain white rice

1 (28-ounce) can diced tomatoes, with juice

3½ cups vegetable broth

¼ teaspoon dried thyme

¼ teaspoon salt, plus more as needed

Black pepper

1. In a large nonstick skillet over medium-high heat, heat 1 tablespoon of the oil. Sauté the sausage for 5 to 7 minutes, until nicely browned. Transfer to a plate.
2. In the same skillet over medium-high heat, heat the remaining 1 tablespoon of oil. Sauté the celery, bell pepper, onion, garlic, and three-quarters of the scallions for 7 to 10 minutes, stirring occasionally, until vegetables are tender.
3. Stir in the rice, tomatoes, broth, sausage, thyme, salt, and pepper to taste. Bring to a boil.
4. Reduce the heat to medium-low, cover the skillet, and simmer for 20 to 25 minutes, until the rice is tender and all the broth is absorbed. Remove from the heat and let rest for 10 minutes, covered. Fluff the rice with a fork. Taste and season with more salt and pepper, as needed. Serve garnished with the remaining scallions.

Fun Fact: *Traditionally, mirepoix is a mix of onion, carrot, and celery. The Cajun and Louisiana Creole variation of mirepoix (called the "holy trinity") is a combination of onion, celery, and green bell pepper.*

Per serving: Calories: 629; Total Fat: 10g; Saturated Fat: 1g; Trans Fat: 0g; Total Carbs: 102g; Fiber: 10g; Protein: 32g; Sodium: 1,537mg; Sugars: 12g

SERVES 4

PREP TIME:
20 minutes

COOK TIME:
1 hour

Mushroom-Lentil Shepherd's Pie

Cremini mushrooms and green lentils step in for meat in this eco-friendly version of the British classic. Also known as "baby bellas," cremini mushrooms have a meaty, deep umami flavor. With the natural complexity of earthy green lentils in this dish, being green has never tasted so good.

GLUTEN-FREE, NUT-FREE, SOY-FREE

1 tablespoon olive oil
2 cups finely diced cremini mushrooms
½ small yellow onion, finely diced
1 small carrot, finely diced
1 small celery stalk, finely diced
1¼ teaspoons salt, divided
½ teaspoon black pepper, divided
1 or 2 garlic cloves, minced
1 cup French green lentils
2 cups vegetable broth
1½ teaspoons herbes de Provence
1 tablespoon tomato paste
⅓ cup frozen peas
2 large (about 1 pound) Yukon Gold or red potatoes, cut into large cubes
½ cup vegan butter or margarine

1. In a medium pot over medium-high heat, heat the oil. Add the mushrooms and sauté for 4 to 5 minutes, until nicely browned. Transfer to a plate.
2. In the same pot, combine the onion, carrot, celery, ¼ teaspoon of the salt, and ¼ teaspoon of the pepper. Sauté for 7 to 10 minutes, stirring occasionally, until the vegetables are tender.
3. Add the garlic, lentils, broth, and herbes de Provence. Bring to a boil. Reduce the heat to low, cover the pot, and simmer for 30 to 35 minutes, until the lentils are tender. Stir in the tomato paste, sautéed mushrooms, and peas.
4. Meanwhile, in a medium saucepan, combine the potatoes and 1 inch of water. Bring to a boil, then cook for 12 to 15 minutes, until the potatoes are tender. Drain, reserving the cooking water, and return the potatoes to the pot. Add the butter and mash well with a potato masher. Add ½ cup of the cooking water and blend. Season with the remaining 1 teaspoon of salt and the remaining ¼ teaspoon of pepper. Add more water, if needed, to get a spreadable consistency.
5. Preheat the broiler to high.
6. Transfer the lentil mixture to a 9-inch square baking dish. Spread the mashed potatoes over the lentil mixture. Place the dish under the broiler for about 5 minutes, or until the potatoes are golden brown. Let rest for 5 minutes before serving..

Per serving: Calories: 524; Total Fat: 28g; Saturated Fat: 15g; Trans Fat: 1g; Total Carbs: 49g; Fiber: 18g; Protein: 17g; Sodium: 1,037mg; Sugars: 4g

Pro Tip: *For a lower-calorie shepherd's pie, swap the potatoes for cauliflower. Cut a cauliflower head into florets and boil for 15 minutes, until tender. Mash or process in a food processor until smooth.*

Loaded English Jacket Potatoes

SERVES 4

PREP TIME: 10 minutes

COOK TIME: about 2 hours

For this recipe, we take a cue from our friends across the pond by slow-roasting our potatoes sans foil to achieve that crisp, almost potato chip–like shell. Once baked, we twice-bake the fluffy centers with vegan butter and cheddar, cashew cream, chives, and tempeh bacon. If you like, you could top the potatoes with Butternut Squash Cheese Sauce (page 129) just before serving. Pair these jacket potatoes with an amber or brown ale or English bitter.

GLUTEN-FREE

4 large russet potatoes

¼ cup vegan butter or margarine

¼ cup Cashew Cream (page 139)

4 tablespoons chopped fresh chives, divided

8 tablespoons shredded vegan cheddar cheese, divided

8 tablespoons crumbled Tempeh Bacon (page 120), divided

Salt and black pepper

1. Preheat the oven to 400°F.
2. Cut a ¼-inch cross on one side of each potato. Bake the potatoes directly on the top oven rack for 1 hour, 30 minutes to 2 hours, until crunchy on the outside and soft on the inside.
3. Cut lengthwise through the top of each baked potato. Scoop the flesh into a large bowl. Add the butter, cashew cream, 1 tablespoon of the chives, 1 tablespoon of the cheddar, and 1 tablespoon of the tempeh bacon. Season with salt and pepper to taste. Spoon the filling into each potato jacket.
4. Sprinkle with the remaining 7 tablespoons of cheddar and return to the oven for 5 minutes, until the cheese melts.
5. Garnish with the remaining 3 tablespoons of chives and 7 tablespoons of bacon.

Pro Tip: *What makes this dish special is the crispy finish of the potato. If that doesn't matter to you, bake your potatoes the traditional American way, pricked with a fork and wrapped in aluminum foil. Bake in the oven for 50 to 60 minutes.*

Per serving (1 potato): Calories: 556; Total Fat: 23g; Saturated Fat: 10g; Trans Fat: 1g; Total Carbs: 73g; Fiber: 8g; Protein: 15g; Sodium: 605mg; Sugars: 4g

MAKES
8 tamales

PREP TIME:
30 minutes, plus
20 minutes to soak

COOK TIME:
40 minutes

Spicy Bean Tamales

A staple across Mexico and the American Southwest, tamales date as far back as 5000 BCE and are a prime example of Mexican communal cooking. During Christmastime, my family made hundreds of tamales for friends and family. Phew, that was a lot of work! Over the years, I've simplified my grandma's traditional—and admittedly tedious—recipe for this easier one that's just as delicious.

GLUTEN-FREE, NUT-FREE, SOY-FREE

8 large corn husks, plus more if needed

1½ cups corn masa flour (masa harina)

½ teaspoon baking powder

½ teaspoon salt

2 tablespoons olive oil

1½ cups warm water

1 recipe Refried Pintos (page 123) or 2 cups store-bought refried beans

1 small jalapeño pepper, seeded and julienned

Cashew Cream (page 139)

Restaurant-Style Chunky Red Salsa (page 136) or store-bought red salsa

1. Soak the corn husks in hot water for 20 minutes. Drain. Using a kitchen towel, pat them dry and reserve in a plastic bag or sealed container until ready to use.
2. In a large bowl, stir together the masa, baking powder, and salt. Add the olive oil. Use your hands to combine the ingredients. Little by little, add the warm water and mix until the batter is a consistent texture.
3. Position a corn husk vertically, with the wide end away from you. Place about ¼ cup of batter in the center of a corn husk. Using the back of a large spoon, spread the batter evenly across the wide/long end of the husk, covering the top two-thirds. Place a spoonful of beans and 2 jalapeño slices in the center of the batter. Gently roll one battered end over the beans, then the second battered end over the other end. The tamale will be rocket-shaped, with a thin, hollow end. Fold up the hollow end, then place on a plate, folded end down; the top remains open. Repeat to make 7 more tamales. In groups of 4, gently tie together the tamales using kitchen twine or strips of corn husks.

4. In a deep medium pot, insert a steamer basket and tightly pack tamales upright on their folded ends. (Tip: Fill empty space in the basket with a heat-resistant mug, leaving room for the steam to circulate.) Add 2 inches of water to the pot, making sure the water line is below the steamer basket. Cover the pot and steam for 30 to 40 minutes, adding more water as needed. Remove from the heat.
5. Uncover the pot and let the tamales sit for 15 minutes, until firm and the tamales easily pull away from the husk. Remove and discard the husks. Serve the tamales warm, with the cashew cream and salsa.

Pro Tip: *Freeze leftover tamales in the husk in an airtight container for up to 6 months. Reheat from frozen. Steam for 25 to 30 minutes.*

Per serving (2 tamales): Calories: 344; Total Fat: 13g; Saturated Fat: 2g; Trans Fat: 0g; Total Carbs: 50g; Fiber: 8g; Protein: 9g; Sodium: 796mg; Sugars: 1g

SERVES 4

PREP TIME:
20 minutes, plus
30 minutes to steep

COOK TIME:
30 minutes

Spanish Chorizo and Vegetable Paella

Paella started as a lunchtime meal for rice-field workers in Valencia's wetlands, who gathered any random ingredients to cook with rice over a woodfire. Once rice became widely available, iterations of the dish were created throughout the Iberian Peninsula. Nowadays, paella is one of the most popular dishes around the world. And this plant-based take on the iconic dish is my ode to Spain, where I spent many summers exploring its gastronomic wonders.

NUT-FREE

- 1 teaspoon saffron threads (see Pro Tip)
- 5 cups vegetable broth
- 3 tablespoons olive oil, divided
- 4 ounces fresh oyster mushrooms, separated
- 2 links Spanish Chorizo (page 106) or store-bought Tofurky kielbasa, cut into ¼-inch slices
- 1 small yellow onion, julienned
- 1 medium red bell pepper, julienned
- 2 or 3 garlic cloves, minced
- 2 ripe Roma (plum) tomatoes, diced
- 1 teaspoon smoked paprika
- 2 cups arborio or short-grain white rice
- ½ teaspoon salt
- 4 canned artichoke hearts
- ½ cup frozen peas
- 1 rosemary sprig

1. In a medium bowl, steep the saffron threads in room-temperature broth for 30 minutes. Strain out the saffron threads and reserve the broth.
2. Heat a paella pan (using natural gas or open flame) or large cast-iron skillet (on a flat stovetop or coils) over medium-high heat. Add 1 tablespoon of the olive oil and the mushrooms. Sauté for 5 to 7 minutes, until nicely browned. Remove from the pan.
3. In the same pan, combine 1 tablespoon of the olive oil and the chorizo. Sauté for 5 to 7 minutes, until nicely browned. Remove from the pan.
4. In the same pan, combine the remaining 1 tablespoon of olive oil, the onion, and bell pepper. Sauté for 4 to 5 minutes, until the onion is translucent. Add the garlic, tomatoes, and smoked paprika. Sauté for 5 to 7 minutes, until the mix caramelizes a bit.
5. Fold in the rice and stir-fry for 1 to 2 minutes.

6. Stir in the mushrooms, chorizo, and salt.
7. Add the saffron broth and give the pan a gentle shake so the rice cooks evenly. Bring to a boil, then reduce the heat to medium-low.
8. Nestle the artichoke hearts in 4 places around the pan. Add the frozen peas and rosemary to the center of the pan. Cook, uncovered, for 20 to 25 minutes, until all the liquid is absorbed and the rice looks fluffy.
9. Increase the heat to medium-high and cook for 1 to 2 minutes more, until the rice on the bottom of the pan is toasted. Remove the rosemary sprig and discard. Serve hot.

Pro Tip: *No saffron? Substitute achiote paste or annatto seeds, which you can find in the international foods aisle of most grocery stores, including Walmart. If using achiote paste, measure ½ teaspoon and stir it into the broth. If using seeds, steep 3 or 4 in the broth for 30 minutes, then remove the seeds before using the broth.*

Per serving: Calories: 438; Total Fat: 13g; Saturated Fat: 2g; Trans Fat: 0g; Total Carbs: 42g; Fiber: 7g; Protein: 28g; Sodium: 1,307mg; Sugars: 7g

Aquafaba Mint-Chocolate Mousse, page 173

CHAPTER ELEVEN

Desserts

Spiced Sweet Potato Cheesecake 168

Texas-Style Pineapple-Mango Cobbler 170

Banana Fudge Pops 171

Coconut Rice Pudding 172

Aquafaba Mint-Chocolate Mousse 173

Spiced Baked Apples with Walnuts and Oats 174

Peanut Butter, Chocolate, and Banana Milk Shake 175

Sweet Quinoa Parfait with Berries and Coconut Flakes 176

Guava Panna Cotta 177

Blueberry Cake Donuts with Meyer Lemon Glaze 178

SERVES 8

PREP TIME:
20 minutes, plus
20 minutes to soak

COOK TIME:
50 minutes, plus
overnight to chill

Spiced Sweet Potato Cheesecake

I've been a fan of cheesecake for as long as I can remember. But as a Southern guy, I've always held a special place in my heart for sweet potato pie, too. So, I decided to marry the two for this spiced holiday dessert. The result is nothing short of a rich, decadent Christmas miracle!

GLUTEN-FREE

FOR THE CRUST

1 cup old-fashioned rolled oats

½ cup raw unsalted almonds

¼ cup sugar

¼ teaspoon salt

3 tablespoons vegan butter or margarine, melted

FOR THE FILLING

1 cup raw unsalted cashews, soaked in hot water for 20 minutes, drained, and rinsed

1 (8-ounce) can unsweetened coconut cream

8 ounces vegan cream cheese

¾ cup agave nectar

½ cup canned sweet potato puree

1 tablespoon tapioca starch or arrowroot starch

1 tablespoon fresh lemon juice

1 teaspoon vanilla extract

¼ teaspoon ground cinnamon

⅛ teaspoon ground ginger

⅛ teaspoon ground nutmeg

⅛ teaspoon ground cloves

⅛ teaspoon salt

1. **Make the crust**: Preheat the oven to 325°F.
2. In a food processor, combine the oats, almonds, sugar, and salt. Process on high speed until you achieve a fine meal. Transfer to a medium bowl. Add the melted butter and use your hands to mix well. Transfer the dough to an 8-inch springform pan, packing it down with a flat object, like the bottom of a glass.
3. **Make the filling:** In a high-speed blender, combine the cashews, coconut cream, cream cheese, agave, sweet potato puree, starch, lemon juice, vanilla, cinnamon, ginger, nutmeg, cloves, and salt. Blend on high speed until very smooth, stopping to scrape down the sides, as needed.
4. Pour the filling into the crust and spread to an even layer. Tap the pan on the table to remove as many air bubbles as possible.

5. Bake for 45 to 50 minutes, until the edges look slightly browned. Let rest for 10 to 15 minutes, then transfer to the refrigerator. Let cool completely, uncovered, overnight.

6. To serve, run a knife dipped in hot water around the edge of the cheesecake to loosen it from the pan. Clean and re-dip the knife, as necessary. Release the side of the pan and lift it away. Cut the cake into 8 even slices.

Pro Tip: *For a tropical cheesecake, replace the sweet potato puree with the same amount of mango puree. Omit the cinnamon, ginger, nutmeg, and cloves, and increase the baking time by 5 minutes.*

Per serving: Calories: 554; Total Fat: 37g; Saturated Fat: 19g; Trans Fat: 0g; Total Carbs: 51g; Fiber: 5g; Protein: 11g; Sodium: 244mg; Sugars: 29g

SERVES 4

PREP TIME: 20 minutes

COOK TIME: 35 minutes

Texas-Style Pineapple-Mango Cobbler

Texans have our own way of doing things—for everything. In most places, cobblers are topped with biscuit dough. In Texas, cobblers are made upside down with a buttery pancake-like batter topped with fruit. This South Texas version features pineapple and mango, a tropical flavor combination that takes me back to those crisp, cool spring break days on sunny South Padre Island.

2 cups diced fresh pineapple

2 large ripe mangos, peeled, cored, and diced

½ cup sugar, divided

¼ teaspoon salt, divided

Grated zest of ½ lemon

Juice of ½ lemon

½ teaspoon ground cinnamon

½ teaspoon vanilla extract

⅔ cup all-purpose flour

1 teaspoon baking powder

½ cup canned unsweetened full-fat coconut milk

¼ cup vegan butter or margarine

1. Preheat the oven to 350°F.
2. In a medium bowl, stir together the pineapple, mango, ¼ cup of the sugar, ⅛ teaspoon of the salt, the lemon zest and juice, cinnamon, and vanilla. Set aside.
3. In another medium bowl, whisk the flour, the remaining ¼ cup of sugar, the remaining ⅛ teaspoon of salt, and the baking powder. Gradually stir in the coconut milk.
4. Put the butter in an 8-inch baking dish and put the dish in the oven for about 5 minutes, until the butter melts, then remove the dish from the oven.
5. In small batches, pour the batter over the butter. Do not stir, and there's no need to cover the entire dish. Evenly place spoonfuls of the pineapple-mango mixture over the batter.
6. Bake for 35 minutes, until the edges are golden brown.

Pro Tip: *The trick to making a perfect Texas-style cobbler is to let the batter fall onto the melted butter and spread to do its own thing. You might be tempted to spread the batter evenly in the pan, but if you do, you'll end up with a wonky, gummy mess.*

Per serving: Calories: 476; Total Fat: 19g; Saturated Fat: 13g; Trans Fat: 1g; Total Carbs: 78g; Fiber: 4g; Protein: 5g; Sodium: 344mg; Sugars: 56g

Banana Fudge Pops

SERVES 4

PREP TIME:
10 minutes, plus
4 hours to freeze

Got overly ripe bananas? That's the first step to making this yummy dessert. The key is to use your ripest bananas and blend them with cocoa powder and full-fat coconut milk. I like to make my fudge pops in the morning so I can enjoy them by lunchtime.

GLUTEN-FREE, OIL-FREE, SOY-FREE

2 ripe bananas, quartered
¼ cup unsweetened cocoa powder
½ cup canned unsweetened full-fat coconut milk
2 tablespoons agave nectar
¼ teaspoon vanilla extract
Pinch salt

In a food processor or blender, add the bananas, cocoa powder, coconut milk, agave nectar, vanilla, and salt and process until very smooth. Transfer the banana-fudge mixture to ice pop molds and seal. Freeze for 4 hours before serving.

Pro Tip: *When I have several ripe bananas, I peel and cut them, then freeze in zip-top plastic bags. Thaw on the kitchen counter for 15 minutes before blending into the mixture.*

Per serving: Calories: 151; Total Fat: 7g; Saturated Fat: 6g; Trans Fat: 0g; Total Carbs: 25g; Fiber: 3g; Protein: 2g; Sodium: 44mg; Sugars: 15g

SERVES 4

PREP TIME:
10 minutes

COOK TIME:
25 minutes

Coconut Rice Pudding

Variations of this warm, creamy dessert can be found in virtually every part of the world with unique spins on ingredients and methods of preparation. It's mentioned in literature from as far back as the Buddhist sutras to modern-day favorites like Dune *and* Harry Potter and the Sorcerer's Stone. *For this plant-based take on the classic, we combine cinnamon-infused rice with coconut milk, vanilla, and golden raisins and top it with toasted coconut flakes.*

GLUTEN-FREE, OIL-FREE, ONE POT, SOY-FREE

2 cups water

2 cinnamon sticks

1 cup arborio rice

1 cup canned unsweetened full-fat coconut milk

¼ cup golden raisins

2 tablespoons sugar

1 teaspoon vanilla extract

¼ teaspoon salt

¼ cup unsweetened coconut flakes, toasted

1. In a medium saucepan, bring the water and cinnamon sticks to a boil. Add the rice and reduce the heat to a low simmer. Cover the pan and cook for about 15 minutes, until the rice is completely cooked.
2. Add the coconut milk and increase the heat to medium.
3. Stir in the raisins, sugar, vanilla, and salt. Cook for 5 minutes, stirring constantly to avoid burning the rice. Serve hot, garnished with the toasted coconut.

Pro Tip: *I love using arborio rice for this recipe because of its plumpness and starchiness, but you can use any short-grain white rice you have on hand.*

Per serving: Calories: 220; Total Fat: 15g; Saturated Fat: 13g; Trans Fat: 0g; Total Carbs: 22g; Fiber: 2g; Protein: 3g; Sodium: 157mg; Sugars: 8g

Aquafaba Mint-Chocolate Mousse

SERVES 4

PREP TIME: 20 minutes

COOK TIME: 5 minutes, plus 20 minutes to cool and 1 hour to chill

One of aquafaba's most magical qualities is its ability to whip up to a stiff foam. For this French-style dessert, we turn to aquafaba to replace the eggs. Melted mint-infused chocolate joins in for a creamy, refreshing dessert.

GLUTEN-FREE, NUT-FREE, SOY-FREE

- 1 cup vegan semisweet chocolate chips
- ¼ teaspoon peppermint extract
- ½ cup aquafaba (from home-cooked or canned chickpeas)
- ⅛ teaspoon cream of tartar
- ¼ cup confectioners' sugar
- 4 fresh mint leaves

1. In a heatproof bowl set above a pan of simmering water, melt the chocolate chips. Whisk in the peppermint extract. Let cool for about 20 minutes.
2. Meanwhile, in a medium bowl, combine the aquafaba and cream of tartar. Using an electric hand mixer, beat for 10 to 15 minutes, until the aquafaba begins to form soft peaks.
3. While continuing to beat, little by little, add the confectioners' sugar.
4. Using a rubber spatula, slowly and gently fold in the mint chocolate until the mix is uniform in texture and color. Transfer the mousse to 4 serving bowls and chill for at least 1 hour. Serve garnished with mint leaves.

Pro Tip: *Whipping the aquafaba can take time, so be patient. If you're not sure whether your aquafaba is stiff enough, it probably isn't—keep going. The great thing about aquafaba is you can't overwhip it, as you can egg whites. If you're lucky enough to own a stand mixer, use it for this.*

Per serving: Calories: 258; Total Fat: 13g; Saturated Fat: 8g; Trans Fat: 0g; Total Carbs: 37g; Fiber: 3g; Protein: 4g; Sodium: 1mg; Sugars: 32g

SERVES 4

PREP TIME:
15 minutes

COOK TIME:
45 minutes, plus
10 minutes to cool

Spiced Baked Apples with Walnuts and Oats

This recipe is an ode to my dear friend Jens and the entire Labusch family in Herten, Germany. It was during my first trip to Germany, at the home of Jens's folks, that I was introduced to this holiday delight, which they called winteräpfel. *Every time I make this sweet, wintry treat, I'm reminded of that wonderful holiday trip across snowy western Germany.*

GLUTEN-FREE

¼ cup chopped walnuts

½ cup old-fashioned rolled oats

½ cup packed dark brown sugar

½ teaspoon vanilla extract

½ teaspoon ground cinnamon

¼ teaspoon ground ginger

⅛ teaspoon ground cloves

Pinch salt

2 tablespoons vegan butter or margarine, melted

4 large crisp red apples (like Honeycrisp, Gala, or Fuji)

⅓ cup apple cider

1. Preheat the oven to 350°F.
2. In a small bowl, stir together the walnuts, oats, brown sugar, vanilla, cinnamon, ginger, cloves, and salt. Add the butter and use your hands to mix everything together.
3. Remove the cores from the apples, making sure not to cut through their base. Place the apples in a 9-inch baking dish and evenly fill them with the oat-walnut mixture. Make sure the apples are tightly packed with the filling.
4. Pour the cider around the apples and cover the dish with aluminum foil.
5. Bake for 15 minutes. Remove the foil and rotate the dish 180 degrees. Bake for 25 to 30 minutes more, until the apples are tender. Let the apples rest for 10 minutes before serving.

Pro Tip: *This holiday dessert is delicious on its own, but I like to add a scoop of vegan vanilla ice cream from time to time for extra indulgence.*

Per serving: Calories: 379; Total Fat: 12g; Saturated Fat: 4g; Trans Fat: 0g; Total Carbs: 66g; Fiber: 7g; Protein: 5g; Sodium: 98mg; Sugars: 46g

Peanut Butter, Chocolate, and Banana Milk Shake

SERVES 4

PREP TIME: 10 minutes

Warning: This lip-smacking milk shake is dangerously addictive! Really—it's so silky and smooth, you'll be fighting your dinner mates for the last drop. For this ice cream–free milk shake, we blend natural peanut butter, ripe bananas, cocoa powder, and full-fat coconut milk to get that classic milk shake mouthfeel. I recommend pulling out the wide straws!

30 MINUTES OR LESS, GLUTEN-FREE, OIL-FREE, ONE POT, SOY-FREE

½ cup unsweetened natural creamy peanut butter

4 ripe bananas, quartered and frozen

2 cups canned unsweetened full-fat coconut milk

¼ cup unsweetened cocoa powder

¼ cup agave nectar

½ teaspoon vanilla extract

⅛ teaspoon salt

1½ cups ice cubes

In a high-speed blender, combine the peanut butter, bananas, coconut milk, cocoa powder, agave nectar, vanilla, salt, and ice cubes. Blend on high speed until smooth. Pour into tall glasses and serve.

Pro Tip: *If you have a peanut allergy, use sunflower seed butter instead of peanut butter.*

Per serving: Calories: 602; Total Fat: 42g; Saturated Fat: 24g; Trans Fat: 0g; Total Carbs: 56g; Fiber: 8g; Protein: 13g; Sodium: 190mg; Sugars: 32g

SERVES 4

PREP TIME: 15 minutes

COOK TIME: 20 minutes

Sweet Quinoa Parfait with Berries and Coconut Flakes

I love quinoa for its versatility. And this protein-packed parfait proves that my favorite super seed has the star power to end any dinner on a sweet note. It's absolutely delightful!

GLUTEN-FREE, OIL-FREE, ONE POT, SOY-FREE

3 cups water

½ teaspoon salt

½ teaspoon ground cinnamon

1½ cups quinoa, rinsed

1 cup quick oats

1 small green apple, peeled, cored, and finely diced

1 cup canned unsweetened full-fat coconut milk

¼ cup packed dark brown sugar

3 cups mixed fresh berries

1 cup unsweetened coconut flakes, toasted

1. In a medium saucepan over medium-high heat, bring the water to a boil. Add the salt, cinnamon, and quinoa. Cover the pan and cook for 15 minutes, until all the water has been absorbed.
2. Stir in the oats, apple, coconut milk, and brown sugar. Cook until heated through.
3. Evenly layer parfait glasses with the berries, coconut flakes, and sweet quinoa mixture.

Pro Tip: *Replace the quinoa with another favorite pseudo-cereal, amaranth. They share a similar nutritional profile, but each has a unique flavor.*

Per serving: Calories: 577; Total Fat: 27g; Saturated Fat: 21g; Trans Fat: 0g; Total Carbs: 77g; Fiber: 15g; Protein: 13g; Sodium: 313mg; Sugars: 26g

Guava Panna Cotta

SERVES 4

PREP TIME: 15 minutes

COOK TIME: 10 minutes, plus 4 hours to chill

Agar-agar is the secret ingredient for making vegan versions of Jell-O–style desserts. Agar-agar is a plant-based gelatin derived from seaweed. You can find it in the international foods section of many grocery stores. In that same section, you'll find guava paste, which gives a Latin twist to this Italian classic, with a perfect custard-like texture.

GLUTEN-FREE, OIL-FREE, SOY-FREE

FOR THE PANNA COTTA

6 tablespoons cold water

¼ cup agar-agar

1 (13.5-ounce) can unsweetened full-fat coconut milk

1 (13.5-ounce) can unsweetened coconut cream

½ cup sugar

½ teaspoon vanilla extract

FOR THE DRESSING

1½ cups water, plus more as needed

7 ounces (half a 14-ounce package) guava paste, cut into small cubes

1. **Make the panna cotta:** In a small bowl, stir together the cold water and agar-agar. Let sit for 5 minutes.
2. In a medium saucepan over medium-high heat, combine the coconut milk, coconut cream, sugar, and vanilla. Bring to a boil.
3. Add the agar-agar mixture and simmer for 1 minute. Transfer to a medium bowl and let cool for 10 minutes.
4. Fill 4 cocktail glasses with the mixture and chill for at least 4 hours.
5. **Make the dressing:** In another saucepan, bring the water to a boil. Stir in the guava paste until you get a syrup consistency, adding more water as needed. Transfer to a small bowl and let cool for 20 minutes before refrigerating.
6. Generously top the chilled panna cotta with the guava syrup. Serve chilled.

Pro Tip: *Replace the guava paste with any fruit topping you like. I also love this dessert with strawberry and blueberry preserves.*

Per serving: Calories: 419; Total Fat: 31g; Saturated Fat: 28g; Trans Fat: 0g; Total Carbs: 35g; Fiber: 4g; Protein: 3g; Sodium: 25mg; Sugars: 29g

MAKES
8 small donuts

PREP TIME:
15 minutes

COOK TIME:
10 minutes, plus 30 minutes to cool and set

Blueberry Cake Donuts with Meyer Lemon Glaze

When I was a kid, I couldn't walk by a Dunkin' Donuts without drooling over the blueberry cake donuts. They were one of the few desserts I really missed when I went vegan. See, Dunkin' uses eggs in its donuts. Womp, womp! Thankfully, I learned a thing or two about baking during my days at the Spiral Diner & Bakery in Dallas. It turns out you don't need eggs to bake donuts! Aquafaba Mayo replaces the egg in these scrumptious blueberry donuts. You'll never need Dunkin' again.

NUT-FREE

FOR THE DONUTS

- 1 cup all-purpose flour
- 1 teaspoon baking powder
- ¼ teaspoon salt
- ⅓ cup soymilk
- 1 teaspoon apple cider vinegar
- 3 tablespoons vegan butter or margarine, melted, plus more to butter pan
- ¼ cup granulated sugar
- 2 tablespoons maple syrup
- 3 tablespoons Aquafaba Mayo (page 141) or store-bought vegan mayo
- ½ cup frozen blueberries, thawed and crushed

FOR THE GLAZE

- ½ cup confectioners' sugar
- 1½ tablespoons fresh Meyer lemon juice
- ½ teaspoon grated Meyer lemon zest

1. **Make the donuts:** Preheat the oven to 400°F.
2. In a medium bowl, stir together the flour, baking powder, and salt.
3. In a small bowl, whisk together the soymilk and vinegar. Let sit for about 5 minutes to curdle.
4. In another small bowl, stir together the melted butter, sugar, and maple syrup. Whisk in the curdled milk. Stir in the mayo and blueberries.
5. Add the wet ingredients to the dry ingredients and stir well.
6. Coat an 8-cup cake donut mold with a little butter. Spoon equal amounts of the batter into the cups.

7. Bake for 8 to 10 minutes, until a toothpick inserted into a donut comes out clean. Cool for 10 minutes, then flip the pan to release the donuts onto a cooling rack. Let cool completely.
8. **Make the glaze:** Place a piece of parchment paper under the cooking rack.
9. In a small bowl, whisk together the confectioners' sugar, lemon juice, and lemon zest until smooth.
10. Dip the top of each donut into the glaze and place upright on the cooling rack until the glaze settles.

Pro Tip: *This recipe calls for frozen blueberries because they're sweeter than fresh blues. Use other frozen berries for variety. Raspberries are a favorite for cake donuts. Use regular lemons if you can't find Meyer lemons.*

Per serving (1 donut): Calories: 195; Total Fat: 9g; Saturated Fat: 3g; Trans Fat: 0g; Total Carbs: 27g; Fiber: 1g; Protein: 2g; Sodium: 190mg; Sugars: 13g

Cashew Cream, page 139

Measurement Conversions

	US STANDARD	US STANDARD (OUNCES)	METRIC (APPROXIMATE)
VOLUME EQUIVALENTS (LIQUID)	2 tablespoons	1 fl. oz.	30 mL
	¼ cup	2 fl. oz.	60 mL
	½ cup	4 fl. oz.	120 mL
	1 cup	8 fl. oz.	240 mL
	1½ cups	12 fl. oz.	355 mL
	2 cups or 1 pint	16 fl. oz.	475 mL
	4 cups or 1 quart	32 fl. oz.	1 L
	1 gallon	128 fl. oz.	4 L
VOLUME EQUIVALENTS (DRY)	⅛ teaspoon		0.5 mL
	¼ teaspoon		1 mL
	½ teaspoon		2 mL
	¾ teaspoon		4 mL
	1 teaspoon		5 mL
	1 tablespoon		15 mL
	¼ cup		59 mL
	⅓ cup		79 mL
	½ cup		118 mL
	⅔ cup		156 mL
	¾ cup		177 mL
	1 cup		235 mL
	2 cups or 1 pint		475 mL
	3 cups		700 mL
	4 cups or 1 quart		1 L
	½ gallon		2 L
	1 gallon		4 L
WEIGHT EQUIVALENTS	½ ounce		15 g
	1 ounce		30 g
	2 ounces		60 g
	4 ounces		115 g
	8 ounces		225 g
	12 ounces		340 g
	16 ounces or 1 pound		455 g

	FAHRENHEIT (F)	CELSIUS (C) (APPROXIMATE)
OVEN TEMPERATURES	250°F	120°F
	300°F	150°C
	325°F	180°C
	375°F	190°C
	400°F	200°C
	425°F	220°C
	450°F	230°C

Resources

Congratulations on completing your first 30 days of vegan eating! Want to dive deeper? Check out these awesome resources.

Cookbooks

Chloe Flavor: Saucy, Crispy, Spicy, Vegan, by Chloe Coscarelli (Clarkson Potter, 2018)

Food Is the Solution: What to Eat to Save the World, by Matthew Prescott (Flatiron Books, 2018)

The Homemade Vegan Pantry: The Art of Making Your Own Staples, by Miyoko Schinner (Ten Speed Press, 2015)

¡Salud! Vegan Mexican Cookbook, by Eddie Garza (Rockridge Press, 2016)

Health and Lifestyle Books

Eat to Live, by Joel Fuhrman, MD (Brown and Co., 2011)

How Not to Die, by Michael Greger, MD (CreateSpace, 2016)

MeatLess, by Kristie Middleton (Da Capo Lifelong Books, 2017)

Lifestyle Websites

Forks Over Knives: ForksOverKnives.com

Happy Cow: HappyCow.net

VegNews magazine: VegNews.com

VegOut magazine: VegOutMag.com

Animal Protection Organizations

Animal Equality: AnimalEquality.org

Farm Sanctuary: FarmSanctuary.org

Mercy for Animals: MercyForAnimals.org

The Humane League: TheHumaneLeague.org

The Humane Society of the United States: HumaneSociety.org

Films

Forks Over Knives

Cowspiracy

The Game Changers

Vegucated

References

Barnard, Neal D., Joshua Cohen, David J. A. Jenkins, Gabrielle Turner-McGrievy, Lise Gloede, Amber Green, and Hope Ferdowsian. "A Low-Fat Vegan Diet and a Conventional Diabetes Diet in the Treatment of Type 2 Diabetes: A Randomized, Controlled, 74-Week Clinical Trial." *American Journal of Clinical Nutrition* 89, no. 5 (May 2009): 1588S–96S. doi.org/10.3945/ajcn.2009.26736H.

Brown, Culum. "Animal Minds: Not Just a Pretty Face." *New Scientist* 2451 (2004): 42–43. NewScientist.com/article/mg18224515-200-animal-minds-not-just-a-pretty-face/?ignored=irrelevant.

Centers for Disease Control and Prevention. "Interactive Atlas of Heart Disease and Stroke." March 13, 2020. CDC.gov/heartdisease/facts.htm#:~:text=Heart%20disease%20is%20the%20leading,1%20in%20every%204%20deaths.

Centers for Disease Control and Prevention. "National Diabetes Statistics Report 2020 Estimates of Diabetes and Its Burden in the United States." 2020: 2. CDC.gov/diabetes/pdfs/data/statistics/national-diabetes-statistics-report.pdf.

Davis, Garth, MD. "Why Does Animal Protein Cause Weight Gain?" *Forks Over Knives*. Published online February 17, 2016. ForksOverKnives.com/wellness/animal-protein-weight-gain/.

Environmental Defense Fund. "Methane: The Other Important Greenhouse Gas." Published online. (n.d.). EDF.org/climate/methane-other-important-greenhouse-gas.

Food and Agriculture Organization of the United Nations. "Key Facts and Findings." (n.d.). FAO.org/news/story/en/item/197623/icode/.

Food and Agriculture Organization of the United Nations. "Water Pollution from Agriculture: A Global Review." 2014. FAO.org/3/a-i7754e.pdf.

Food and Agriculture Organization of the United Nations. "The State of the World's Forests." 2020. FAO.org/state-of-forests/en/.

Grossman-Cohen, Ben. CNN. "'Meatless Monday' Too Hot a Potato for USDA." CNN Opinion. August 12, 2012. CNN.com/2012/08/02/opinion/grossman-cohen-meatless-monday/index.html.

Hales, C. M., M. D. Carroll, C. D. Fryar, and C. L. Ogden. "Prevalence of Obesity and Severe Obesity among Adults: United States, 2017–2018." NCHS Data Brief no. 360 (2020). Hyattsville, MD: National Center for Health Statistics. CDC.gov/nchs/products/databriefs/db360.htm.

Institute of Medicine. Food and Nutrition Board. *Dietary Reference Intakes for Vitamin A, Vitamin K, Arsenic, Boron, Chromium, Copper, Iodine, Iron, Manganese, Molybdenum, Nickel, Silicon, Vanadium, and Zinc: A Report of the Panel on Micronutrients*. Washington, DC: National Academy Press, 2001. NAP.edu/read/10026/chapter/1#vi.

IPCC Core Writing Team, R. K. Pachauri, and L. A. Meyer (eds.). "Climate Change 2014: Synthesis Report." Contribution of Working Groups I, II, and III to the Fifth Assessment Report of the Intergovernmental Panel on Climate Change. IPCC, Geneva, Switzerland. (2014): 151. IPCC.ch/report/ar5/syr/.

Marino, Lori. "Thinking Chickens: A Review of Cognition, Emotion, and Behavior in the Domestic Chicken." *Animal Cognition* 20 (2017): 27–147. doi:10.1007/s10071-016-1064-4.

National Institutes of Health. Office of Dietary Supplements. "Calcium Fact Sheet for Consumers." Updated online December 6, 2019. ODS.od.nih.gov/factsheets/Calcium-HealthProfessional/.

National Institutes of Health. Office of Dietary Supplements. "Omega-3 Fatty Acids." ODS.od.nih.gov/factsheets/Omega3FattyAcids-HealthProfessional/#:~:text=In%20adults%20aged%2020%20and,in%20adults)%20%5B39%5D.

National Institutes of Health. Office of Dietary Supplements. "Vitamin B_{12} Fact Sheet for Consumers." Updated online March 30, 2020. ODS.od.nih.gov/factsheets/VitaminB12-Consumer/#:~:text=Vitamin%20B12%20is%20a%20nutrient,makes%20people%20tired%20and%20weak.

Physicians Committee for Responsible Medicine. "Cancer: Reducing Cancer Risk with a Plant-Based Diet." Published online. (n.d.). PCRM.org/health-topics/cancer.

Physicians Committee for Responsible Medicine. "Colorectal Cancer: Fight Colorectal Cancer with a Plant-Based Diet." Published online. (n.d.). PCRM.org/health-topics/colorectal-cancer.

Physicians Committee for Responsible Medicine. "Heart Disease: Boost Heart Health with a Plant-Based Diet." (n.d.). PCRM.org/health-topics/heart-disease.

Tantamango-Bartley, T., S. F. Knutsen, R. Knutsen, et al. "Are Strict Vegetarians Protected against Prostate Cancer?" *The American Journal of Clinical Nutrition* 103, no. 1 (January 2016): 153–60. doi:10.3945/ajcn.114.106450.

US Department of Agriculture, Agricultural Research Service. "What We Eat in America, 2009–2010." 2012. ARS.usda.gov/northeast-area/beltsville-md-bhnrc/beltsville-human-nutrition-research-center/food-surveys-research-group/docs/main-service-page/.

US Department of Agriculture, Agricultural Research Service. "What We Eat in America, 2011–2012." 2015. ARS.usda.gov/northeast-area/beltsville-md-bhnrc/beltsville-human-nutrition-research-center/food-surveys-research-group/docs/main-service-page/.

US Geological Survey. "The Water Content of Things: How Much Water Does It Take to Grow a Hamburger?" Updated online December 22, 2016. Water.usgs.gov/edu/activity-watercontent.php.

The Vegan Society. "What is Veganism?" November 18, 2020. Vegansociety.com/about-us/further-information/key-facts.

World Cancer Research Fund International/American Institute for Cancer Research. *Diet, Nutrition, Physical Activity and Cancer: A Global Perspective.* Continuous Update Project Report 2018. WCRF.org/sites/default/files/Recommendations.pdf.

Zhang, F. F., D. E. Haslam, M. B. Terry, et al. "Dietary Isoflavone Intake and All-Cause Mortality in Breast Cancer Survivors: The Breast Cancer Family Registry." *Cancer* 123, no. 11 (2017): 2070–79. doi:10.1002/cncr.30615.

General Index

A

Agave-Chipotle Vinaigrette, 127
All-American Black Bean Burgers, 92–93
Almond milk, 21
Almonds
  Spiced Sweet Potato Cheesecake, 168–169
Amaranth-Quinoa Porridge with Dried Cranberries and Pumpkin Seeds, 57
Apples
  Apple-Sage Andouille Sausage, 109
  Frisée and Apple Salad with Walnuts and Pomegranate, 69
  Spiced Baked Apples with Walnuts and Oats, 174
  Tofu Chops with Caramelized Apple and Onion, 151
Aquafaba
  about, 23
  Aquafaba Mayo, 141
  Aquafaba Mint-Chocolate Mousse, 173
Arugula, Baby, and Macadamia Ricotta, Roasted Beet Salad with, 70
Avocados
  Avocado Toast-adas, 63
  Berry Superfood Smoothie Bowls, 58
  Caribbean Island Burgers with Mango Relish, 98
  Caribbean Jerk Tempeh Bowls, 154
  Easy Guacamole, 111
  Gallo Pinto (Central American Rice and Beans), 146
  Mango Shiitake Ceviche, 76
  Portobello-Pineapple Poke Bowls, 147
  Southwestern Black Bean and Quinoa Bowls, 144
  Tex-Mex Taco Salad, 74
  Tex-Mex Tortilla Soup, 85
  Tropical Quinoa Salad, 71

B

Baked Barbecue Cauliflower Wings, 115
Balsamic Reduction, 137
Bananas
  Banana Fudge Pops, 171
  Berry Superfood Smoothie Bowls, 58
  Blueberry Oatmeal with Walnuts, Banana, and Coconut, 59
  Peanut Butter, Chocolate, and Banana Milk Shake, 175
Barbecue Sauce, Texas-Style, 134
Basil
  Basil Pesto, 133
  Crostini with Macadamia Ricotta, Strawberries, and Basil, 110
Beans. *See also* Chickpeas; Edamame
  All-American Black Bean Burgers, 92–93
  Apple-Sage Andouille Sausage, 109
  Avocado Toast-adas, 63
  Caribbean Island Burgers with Mango Relish, 98
  Caribbean Jerk Tempeh Bowls, 154
  Easy Three-Bean Chili, 86
  Gallo Pinto (Central American Rice and Beans), 146
  Italian Sausage, 108
  Quick Cuban Black Bean Soup, 88
  Refried Pintos, 123
  Southwestern Black Bean and Quinoa Bowls, 144
  Spanish Chorizo, 106–107
  Spicy Bean Tamales, 162–163
  Thick and Hearty Minestrone, 84
  Tropical Quinoa Salad, 71
Beets
  Roasted Beet Salad with Baby Arugula and Macadamia Ricotta, 70
  Rustic Roasted Root Vegetables, 121

Berries
Berry Superfood Smoothie Bowls, 58
Blueberry Cake Donuts with Meyer Lemon Glaze, 178–179
Blueberry Oatmeal with Walnuts, Banana, and Coconut, 59
Crostini with Macadamia Ricotta, Strawberries, and Basil, 110
Quinoa-Amaranth Porridge with Dried Cranberries and Pumpkin Seeds, 57
Sweet Quinoa Parfait with Berries and Coconut Flakes, 176
Blender, 24
Blueberries
Berry Superfood Smoothie Bowls, 58
Blueberry Cake Donuts with Meyer Lemon Glaze, 178–179
Blueberry Oatmeal with Walnuts, Banana, and Coconut, 59
Breakfast
Avocado Toast-adas, 63
Berry Superfood Smoothie Bowls, 58
Blueberry Oatmeal with Walnuts, Banana, and Coconut, 59
Easy Overnight Oats, 60
Fried Tofu Eggs, 55
Portobello Steak and Tofu Eggs with Oven Home Fries, 64
Quinoa-Amaranth Porridge with Dried Cranberries and Pumpkin Seeds, 57
Scrambled Tofu Eggs, 54
Tex-Mex Migas, 61
Tex-Mex Tofu Scramble, 55–56
Tofu Egg Sandwiches, 65
Tofu Eggs Benedict with Tempeh Bacon, Wilted Spinach, and Cashew Hollandaise, 62
Broccoli
Broccoli with Butternut Squash Cheese Sauce, 117
Cream of Broccoli Soup, 82
Grilled Tofu and Veggie Kabobs with Chimichurri Sauce, 116
Broiler chickens, 7
Broths, stocking up on, 20
Brussels sprouts
Chopped Fall Salad with Herbs, 73
Burgers
All-American Black Bean Burgers, 92–93
Caribbean Island Burgers with Mango Relish, 98
Butter, vegan, buying, 20–21

Cabbage, Napa, Salad, 72
Caesar Dressing, Cashew, 128
Caesar Salad with Italian-Herbed Roasted Chickpeas, 75
Calcium, 15
Cancer, 12–13
Caribbean Island Burgers with Mango Relish, 98
Caribbean Jerk Tempeh Bowls, 154
Carrots
Hearty Vegetable Stew, 89
Napa Cabbage Salad, 72
Portobello-Pineapple Poke Bowls, 147
Rustic Roasted Root Vegetables, 121
Tofu Summer Rolls, 113
Cashew milk, 21
Cashews
Butternut Squash Cheese Sauce, 129
Cashew Caesar Dressing, 128
Cashew Cream, 139
Cashew Hollandaise, 135
Cashew Mozzarella and Marinara Dip, 112
Spiced Sweet Potato Cheesecake, 168–169
Cauliflower
Baked Barbecue Cauliflower Wings, 115
Crispy Cauliflower Po' Boys, 100–101
Grilled Tofu and Veggie Kabobs with Chimichurri Sauce, 116
as meat alternative, 25
Ceviche, Mango Shiitake, 76
Chana Masala, Easy, 156
Cheese, vegan
All-American Black Bean Burgers, 92–93
buying, 21
French Onion Soup, 80
Grilled Vegetable Panini with Basil Pesto, 97

Italian Seitan Sausage Hoagies, 96
Loaded English Jacket Potatoes, 161
Spiced Sweet Potato Cheesecake, 168–169
Tex-Mex Taco Salad, 74
Tex-Mex Tortilla Soup, 85
Tofu Egg Sandwiches, 65
Cheesecake, Spiced Sweet Potato, 168–169
Chef's knife, 24
Chickens, 7
Chickpeas
Caesar Salad with Italian-Herbed Roasted Chickpeas, 75
Classic Chick-Free Salad, 77
Easy Chana Masala, 156
Italian-Herbed Roasted Chickpeas, 114
as meat alternative, 25
Chili, Easy Three-Bean, 86
Chimichurri Sauce, 140
Chocolate
Aquafaba Mint-Chocolate Mousse, 173
Banana Fudge Pops, 171
Peanut Butter, Chocolate, and Banana Milk Shake, 175
Chopped Fall Salad with Herbs, 73
Classic Chick-Free Salad, 77
Climate change, 5
Cobbler, Texas-Style Pineapple-Mango, 170
Coconut
Berry Superfood Smoothie Bowls, 58
Blueberry Oatmeal with Walnuts, Banana, and Coconut, 59
Coconut Rice Pudding, 172
Sweet Quinoa Parfait with Berries and Coconut Flakes, 176
Tropical Quinoa Salad, 71
Corn
Avocado Toast-adas, 63
Southwestern Black Bean and Quinoa Bowls, 144
Tex-Mex Tofu Scramble, 55–56
Tex-Mex Tortilla Soup, 85
Wild Mushroom and Vegetable Fried Rice, 155
Cows, 6–7
Cranberries, Dried, and Pumpkin Seeds, Quinoa-Amaranth Porridge with, 57
Cream of Broccoli Soup, 82
Crispy Cauliflower Po' Boys, 100–101
Crostini with Macadamia Ricotta, Strawberries, and Basil, 110
Cucumbers
Napa Cabbage Salad, 72
Portobello-Pineapple Poke Bowls, 147
Tofu Summer Rolls, 113
Watermelon, Cucumber, and Mint Salad, 68
Watermelon-Mint Gazpacho, 83

D

Dairy factory farms, 6–7
Deforestation, 6
Desserts
Aquafaba Mint-Chocolate Mousse, 173
Banana Fudge Pops, 171
Blueberry Cake Donuts with Meyer Lemon Glaze, 178–179
Coconut Rice Pudding, 172
Guava Panna Cotta, 177
Peanut Butter, Chocolate, and Banana Milk Shake, 175
Spiced Baked Apples with Walnuts and Oats, 174
Spiced Sweet Potato Cheesecake, 168–169
Sweet Quinoa Parfait with Berries and Coconut Flakes, 176
Texas-Style Pineapple-Mango Cobbler, 170
Diabetes, 12
Dining out, 28
Dips
Cashew Mozzarella and Marinara Dip, 112
Easy Guacamole, 111
Donuts, Blueberry Cake, with Meyer Lemon Glaze, 178–179
Dressings
Agave-Chipotle Vinaigrette, 127
Balsamic Reduction, 137
Cashew Caesar Dressing, 128
Maple-Cinnamon Vinaigrette, 126
Red Wine Vinaigrette, 126

E

Easy Chana Masala, 156
Easy Guacamole, 111
Easy Overnight Oats, 60
Easy Three-Bean Chili, 86
Edamame
 Portobello-Pineapple Poke Bowls, 147
 Wild Mushroom and Vegetable Fried Rice, 155
Egg alternatives, 22–23
Eggplant
 Grilled Vegetable Panini with Basil Pesto, 97
Electric pressure cooker, 24
Equipment, 24

F

Fajitas, Seared Portobello, 153
Fiber, 13
Fish, 8
Flatbread, Herbed Oyster Mushroom White Cream, 158
Flax eggs, 23
Flax meal, 23
Flexitarians, 5
Food labels, 27
Food shopping, 27
French Onion Soup, 80
Fried Tofu Eggs, 55
Frisée and Apple Salad with Walnuts and Pomegranate, 69
Fruit. *See* Berries; *specific fruits*
Fudge Pops, Banana, 171

G

Gallo Pinto (Central American Rice and Beans), 146
Gazpacho, Watermelon-Mint, 83
Grains. *See also* Oats; Quinoa; Rice
 Quinoa-Amaranth Porridge with Dried Cranberries and Pumpkin Seeds, 57
 stocking up on, 20
Greens
 Caesar Salad with Italian-Herbed Roasted Chickpeas, 75
 Chopped Fall Salad with Herbs, 73
 Frisée and Apple Salad with Walnuts and Pomegranate, 69
 Portobello-Pineapple Poke Bowls, 147
 Roasted Beet Salad with Baby Arugula and Macadamia Ricotta, 70
 Tempeh BLTs, 103
 Tex-Mex Tofu Scramble, 55–56
 Tofu Eggs Benedict with Tempeh Bacon, Wilted Spinach, and Cashew Hollandaise, 62
Grilled Tofu and Veggie Kabobs with Chimichurri Sauce, 116
Grilled Vegetable Panini with Basil Pesto, 97
Grocery shopping, 27
Guacamole, Easy, 111
Guava Panna Cotta, 177

H

Heart health, 11–12
Hearty Vegetable Stew, 89
Herbs. *See also specific*
 Chimichurri Sauce, 140
 Chopped Fall Salad with Herbs, 73
 Herbed Oyster Mushroom White Cream Flatbread, 158
High-speed blender, 24
Hoagies, Italian Seitan Sausage, 96
Hollandaise, Cashew, 135
Home Fries, Oven, 118

I

Iron, 15
Italian-Herbed Roasted Chickpeas, 114
Italian Sausage, 108
Italian Seitan Sausage Hoagies, 96

J

Jackfruit
 Jackfruit Barbecue Sandwiches, 99
 as meat alternative, 25
Jambalaya, Seitan Sausage, 159
Jerk Tempeh Bowls, Caribbean, 154

K

Kale
  Chopped Fall Salad with Herbs, 73
Knives, 24

L

Laying hens, 7
Lentils
  Lentil Sloppy Joes, 94
  Mom's Homestyle Lentil Soup, 81
  Mushroom-Lentil Shepherd's Pie, 160
  Wild Rice and Lentil Stuffed Acorn Squash, 150
Lettuce
  Caesar Salad with Italian-Herbed Roasted Chickpeas, 75
  Tempeh BLTs, 103
Loaded English Jacket Potatoes, 161

M

Macadamia nuts
  Crostini with Macadamia Ricotta, Strawberries, and Basil, 110
  Macadamia-Cashew Carbonara with Tempeh Bacon, 157
  Roasted Beet Salad with Baby Arugula and Macadamia Ricotta, 70
Mac and Cheese, Butternut Squash, 152
Mangos
  Caribbean Island Burgers with Mango Relish, 98
  Mango Relish, 138
  Mango Shiitake Ceviche, 76
  Texas-Style Pineapple-Mango Cobbler, 170
Maple-Cinnamon Vinaigrette, 126
Marinara, 20-Minute, 132
Marinara and Cashew Mozzarella Dip, 112
Mayo, Aquafaba, 141
Meal plan, 28–37
Meat alternatives, 25–26
Migas, Tex-Mex, 61
Milks, vegan, 21–22
Milk Shake, Peanut Butter, Chocolate, and Banana, 175
Minestrone, Thick and Hearty, 84
Mint
  Aquafaba Mint-Chocolate Mousse, 173
  Watermelon, Cucumber, and Mint Salad, 68
  Watermelon-Mint Gazpacho, 83
Mom's Homestyle Lentil Soup, 81
Mousse, Aquafaba Mint-Chocolate, 173
Mushrooms
  Grilled Tofu and Veggie Kabobs with Chimichurri Sauce, 116
  Grilled Vegetable Panini with Basil Pesto, 97
  Herbed Oyster Mushroom White Cream Flatbread, 158
  Mango Shiitake Ceviche, 76
  as meat alternative, 25–26
  Mushroom-Lentil Shepherd's Pie, 160
  Portobello-Pineapple Poke Bowls, 147
  Portobello Steak and Chimichurri Sandwiches, 95
  Portobello Steak and Tofu Eggs with Oven Home Fries, 64
  Seared Oyster Mushroom Tortas, 102
  Seared Portobello Fajitas, 153
  Spanish Chorizo and Vegetable Paella, 164–165
  Sweet Potato and Shiitake Mushroom Risotto, 148
  Tex-Mex Tortilla Soup, 85
  Wild Mushroom and Vegetable Fried Rice, 155
  Wild Rice and Lentil Stuffed Acorn Squash, 150

N

Napa Cabbage Salad, 72
Nutritional yeast, about, 22
Nutrition basics, 15–17
Nuts. *See also* Cashews
  Basil Pesto, 133
  Blueberry Oatmeal with Walnuts, Banana, and Coconut, 59
  Chopped Fall Salad with Herbs, 73
  Crostini with Macadamia Ricotta, Strawberries, and Basil, 110

Nuts (*continued*)
Frisée and Apple Salad with Walnuts and Pomegranate, 69
Macadamia-Cashew Carbonara with Tempeh Bacon, 157
Roasted Beet Salad with Baby Arugula and Macadamia Ricotta, 70
Spiced Baked Apples with Walnuts and Oats, 174
Spiced Sweet Potato Cheesecake, 168–169
stocking up on, 20
Wild Rice and Lentil Stuffed Acorn Squash, 150

O

Oat milk, 22
Oats
Berry Superfood Smoothie Bowls, 58
Blueberry Oatmeal with Walnuts, Banana, and Coconut, 59
Easy Overnight Oats, 60
Spiced Baked Apples with Walnuts and Oats, 174
Spiced Sweet Potato Cheesecake, 168–169
Sweet Quinoa Parfait with Berries and Coconut Flakes, 176
Obesity, 13
Omega-3 fatty acids, 16
Onions
French Onion Soup, 80
Tofu Chops with Caramelized Apple and Onion, 151
Oven Home Fries, 118

P

Paella, Spanish Chorizo and Vegetable, 164–165
Panna Cotta, Guava, 177
Pan-Sautéed Sweet Plantains, 119
Parfait, Sweet Quinoa, with Berries and Coconut Flakes, 176
Parsley
Chimichurri Sauce, 140
Pasta and noodles
Butternut Squash Mac and Cheese, 152
Macadamia-Cashew Carbonara with Tempeh Bacon, 157
Pasta Bolognese, 145
Thick and Hearty Minestrone, 84
Tofu Summer Rolls, 113
Peanut butter
Peanut Butter, Chocolate, and Banana Milk Shake, 175
Peanut Sauce, 131
Pears
Chopped Fall Salad with Herbs, 73
Peas
Hearty Vegetable Stew, 89
Mushroom-Lentil Shepherd's Pie, 160
Spanish Chorizo and Vegetable Paella, 164–165
Peppers
Caribbean Jerk Tempeh Bowls, 154
Grilled Tofu and Veggie Kabobs with Chimichurri Sauce, 116
Grilled Vegetable Panini with Basil Pesto, 97
Italian Seitan Sausage Hoagies, 96
Mango Shiitake Ceviche, 76
Napa Cabbage Salad, 72
Seared Portobello Fajitas, 153
Spanish Chorizo and Vegetable Paella, 164–165
Tex-Mex Tofu Scramble, 55–56
Tofu Summer Rolls, 113
Watermelon-Mint Gazpacho, 83
Pesto, Basil, 133
Phytochemicals, 13
Pigs, 7
Pineapple
Portobello-Pineapple Poke Bowls, 147
Texas-Style Pineapple-Mango Cobbler, 170
Tropical Quinoa Salad, 71
Pine nuts
Basil Pesto, 133
Chopped Fall Salad with Herbs, 73
Pitts, Lauren, 28–29
Plantains
Caribbean Island Burgers with Mango Relish, 98
Caribbean Jerk Tempeh Bowls, 154
Pan-Sautéed Sweet Plantains, 119

Po' Boys, Crispy Cauliflower, 100–101
Poke Bowls, Portobello-Pineapple, 147
Pomegranate and Walnuts, Frisée and Apple Salad with, 69
Porridge, Quinoa-Amaranth, with Dried Cranberries and Pumpkin Seeds, 57
Potatoes. *See also* Sweet potatoes
- Hearty Vegetable Stew, 89
- Loaded English Jacket Potatoes, 161
- Mushroom-Lentil Shepherd's Pie, 160
- Oven Home Fries, 118
- Rustic Roasted Root Vegetables, 121

Protein, vegan, 17
Pudding, Coconut Rice, 172
Pumpkin seeds
- Avocado Toast-adas, 63
- Berry Superfood Smoothie Bowls, 58
- Quinoa-Amaranth Porridge with Dried Cranberries and Pumpkin Seeds, 57
- Southwestern Black Bean and Quinoa Bowls, 144

Q

Quick Cuban Black Bean Soup, 88
Quinoa
- Quinoa-Amaranth Porridge with Dried Cranberries and Pumpkin Seeds, 57
- Southwestern Black Bean and Quinoa Bowls, 144
- Sweet Quinoa Parfait with Berries and Coconut Flakes, 176
- Tropical Quinoa Salad, 71

R

Radicchio
- Chopped Fall Salad with Herbs, 73

Reducitarians, 5
Red Wine Vinaigrette, 126
Refried Pintos, 123
Relish, Mango, 138
Rémoulade Sauce, 100
Restaurant-Style Chunky Red Salsa, 136
Rice
- Caribbean Jerk Tempeh Bowls, 154
- Coconut Rice Pudding, 172
- Gallo Pinto (Central American Rice and Beans), 146
- Portobello-Pineapple Poke Bowls, 147
- Seitan Sausage Jambalaya, 159
- Spanish Chorizo and Vegetable Paella, 164–165
- Spanish Rice, 122
- Sweet Potato and Shiitake Mushroom Risotto, 148
- Wild Mushroom and Vegetable Fried Rice, 155
- Wild Rice and Lentil Stuffed Acorn Squash, 150

Risotto, Sweet Potato and Shiitake Mushroom, 148
Roasted Beet Salad with Baby Arugula and Macadamia Ricotta, 70
Roasted Butternut Squash Soup, 87
Rustic Roasted Root Vegetables, 121

S

Salad dressings, vegan, 22
Salads
- Caesar Salad with Italian-Herbed Roasted Chickpeas, 75
- Chopped Fall Salad with Herbs, 73
- Classic Chick-Free Salad, 77
- Frisée and Apple Salad with Walnuts and Pomegranate, 69
- Mango Shiitake Ceviche, 76
- Napa Cabbage Salad, 72
- Roasted Beet Salad with Baby Arugula and Macadamia Ricotta, 70
- Tex-Mex Taco Salad, 74
- Tropical Quinoa Salad, 71
- Watermelon, Cucumber, and Mint Salad, 68

Salsa
- Restaurant-Style Chunky Red Salsa, 136
- Salsa Fresca, 130

Sandwiches
- Crispy Cauliflower Po' Boys, 100–101
- Grilled Vegetable Panini with Basil Pesto, 97
- Italian Seitan Sausage Hoagies, 96

Sandwiches (*continued*)
Jackfruit Barbecue Sandwiches, 99
Lentil Sloppy Joes, 94
Portobello Steak and Chimichurri Sandwiches, 95
Seared Oyster Mushroom Tortas, 102
Tempeh BLTs, 103
Tofu Egg Sandwiches, 65
Sauces
Aquafaba Mayo, 141
Basil Pesto, 133
Butternut Squash Cheese Sauce, 129
Cashew Cream, 139
Cashew Hollandaise, 135
Chimichurri Sauce, 140
Peanut Sauce, 131
Rémoulade, 100
Texas-Style Barbecue Sauce, 134
20-Minute Marinara, 132
Scrambled Tofu Eggs, 54
Seared Oyster Mushroom Tortas, 102
Seeds. *See also* Pumpkin seeds
stocking up on, 20
Seitan sausage
Apple-Sage Andouille Sausage, 109
Italian Sausage, 108
Italian Seitan Sausage Hoagies, 96
as meat alternative, 26
Pasta Bolognese, 145
Seitan Chorizo Tacos, 149
Seitan Sausage Jambalaya, 159
Spanish Chorizo, 106–107
Spanish Chorizo and Vegetable Paella, 164–165
Tex-Mex Taco Salad, 74
Shepherd's Pie, Mushroom-Lentil, 160
Shopping lists, 38–49
Sloppy Joes, Lentil, 94
Smoothie Bowls, Berry Superfood, 58
Soups
Cream of Broccoli Soup, 82
French Onion Soup, 80
Mom's Homestyle Lentil Soup, 81
Quick Cuban Black Bean Soup, 88
Roasted Butternut Squash Soup, 87
Tex-Mex Tortilla Soup, 85
Thick and Hearty Minestrone, 84
Watermelon-Mint Gazpacho, 83
Sour cream, vegan, 21
Southwestern Black Bean and Quinoa Bowls, 144
Soymilk, 22
Spanish Chorizo, 106–107
Spanish Rice, 122
Spiced Baked Apples with Walnuts and Oats, 174
Spiced Sweet Potato Cheesecake, 168–169
Spicy Bean Tamales, 162–163
Spinach
Tex-Mex Tofu Scramble, 55–56
Tofu Eggs Benedict with Tempeh Bacon, Wilted Spinach, and Cashew Hollandaise, 62
Squash
Broccoli with Butternut Squash Cheese Sauce, 117
Butternut Squash Cheese Sauce, 129
Butternut Squash Mac and Cheese, 152
Grilled Vegetable Panini with Basil Pesto, 97
Roasted Butternut Squash Soup, 87
Thick and Hearty Minestrone, 84
Wild Rice and Lentil Stuffed Acorn Squash, 150
Stews
Easy Three-Bean Chili, 86
Hearty Vegetable Stew, 89
Stocks, for recipes, 20
Strawberries
Berry Superfood Smoothie Bowls, 58
Crostini with Macadamia Ricotta, Strawberries, and Basil, 110
Summer Rolls, Tofu, 113
Sunlight exposure, 16
Sweet potatoes
Rustic Roasted Root Vegetables, 121
Spiced Sweet Potato Cheesecake, 168–169
Sweet Potato and Shiitake Mushroom Risotto, 148

T

Tacos, Seitan Chorizo, 149
Taco Salad, Tex-Mex, 74
Tamales, Spicy Bean, 162–163
Tempeh. *See also* Tempeh Bacon
  about, 26
  Caribbean Jerk Tempeh Bowls, 154
Tempeh Bacon
  Caesar Salad with Italian-Herbed Roasted Chickpeas, 75
  Loaded English Jacket Potatoes, 161
  Macadamia-Cashew Carbonara with Tempeh Bacon, 157
  recipe for, 120
  Tempeh BLTs, 103
  Tofu Egg Sandwiches, 65
  Tofu Eggs Benedict with Tempeh Bacon, Wilted Spinach, and Cashew Hollandaise, 62
Texas-Style Barbecue Sauce, 134
Texas-Style Pineapple-Mango Cobbler, 170
Tex-Mex Migas, 61
Tex-Mex Taco Salad, 74
Tex-Mex Tofu Scramble, 55–56
Tex-Mex Tortilla Soup, 85
Thick and Hearty Minestrone, 84
Toast-adas, Avocado, 63
Tofu
  as egg alternative, 23
  Fried Tofu Eggs, 55
  Grilled Tofu and Veggie Kabobs with Chimichurri Sauce, 116
  as meat alternative, 26
  Portobello Steak and Tofu Eggs with Oven Home Fries, 64
  Scrambled Tofu Eggs, 54
  Tex-Mex Migas, 61
  Tex-Mex Tofu Scramble, 55–56
  Tofu Chops with Caramelized Apple and Onion, 151
  Tofu Egg Sandwiches, 65
  Tofu Eggs Benedict with Tempeh Bacon, Wilted Spinach, and Cashew Hollandaise, 62
  Tofu Summer Rolls, 113
Tofu press, 24
Tomatoes
  Easy Chana Masala, 156
  Easy Three-Bean Chili, 86
  Hearty Vegetable Stew, 89
  Restaurant-Style Chunky Red Salsa, 136
  Salsa Fresca, 130
  Seitan Sausage Jambalaya, 159
  Tempeh BLTs, 103
  Texas-Style Barbecue Sauce, 134
  Tex-Mex Taco Salad, 74
  Tex-Mex Tofu Scramble, 55–56
  Tex-Mex Tortilla Soup, 85
  Thick and Hearty Minestrone, 84
  20-Minute Marinara, 132
  Watermelon-Mint Gazpacho, 83
Tortas, Seared Oyster Mushroom, 102
Tortillas
  Seared Portobello Fajitas, 153
  Seitan Chorizo Tacos, 149
  Tex-Mex Migas, 61
  Tex-Mex Tortilla Soup, 85
Tropical Quinoa Salad, 71
Turkeys, 8
20-Minute Marinara, 132
Type 2 diabetes, 12

V

Vegan diet
  author's story, 14
  benefits for animal life, 6–8
  calcium-rich foods, 15
  for cancer risk reduction, 12–13
  compared to vegetarian diet, 4–5
  dairy alternatives, 20–22
  for diabetes prevention, 12
  dining out options, 28
  egg alternatives, 22–23
  environmental benefits, 5–6
  heart health benefits, 11–12
  helpful equipment for, 24
  iron-rich foods, 15
  meal plan for, 28–37

Vegan diet (*continued*)
meal plan shopping lists, 38–49
meat alternatives, 25–26
nutrition basics, 15–17
omega-3 fatty acids for, 16
overview, 3–4
pantry staples, 19–20
protein for, 17
shopping for groceries, 27
vitamin B12 for, 16
vitamin D for, 16–17
for weight management, 13
zinc for, 17
Veganism, definition of, 4
Vegetables. *See also specific vegetables*
Grilled Vegetable Panini with Basil Pesto, 97
Hearty Vegetable Stew, 89
Rustic Roasted Root Vegetables, 121
Vegetarian diet, 4–5
Vinaigrettes
Agave-Chipotle Vinaigrette, 127
Maple-Cinnamon Vinaigrette, 126
Red Wine Vinaigrette, 126
Vital wheat gluten
about, 26
Seitan Sausage 3 Ways, 106–109
Vitamin B12, 16
Vitamin C, 15
Vitamin D, 16–17

W

Walnuts
Blueberry Oatmeal with Walnuts, Banana, and Coconut, 59
Frisée and Apple Salad with Walnuts and Pomegranate, 69
Spiced Baked Apples with Walnuts and Oats, 174
Wild Rice and Lentil Stuffed Acorn Squash, 150
Watermelon
Watermelon, Cucumber, and Mint Salad, 68
Watermelon-Mint Gazpacho, 83
Water pollution, 5–6
Weight management, 13
Wild Rice and Lentil Stuffed Acorn Squash, 150

Y

Yogurt, coconut
Easy Overnight Oats, 60

Z

Zinc, 17
Zucchini
Grilled Vegetable Panini with Basil Pesto, 97
Thick and Hearty Minestrone, 84

Recipe Index by Nutrition Label

Gluten-free

Agave-Chipotle Vinaigrette, 127
Aquafaba Mayo, 141
Aquafaba Mint-Chocolate Mousse, 173
Avocado Toast-adas, 63
Balsamic Reduction, 137
Banana Fudge Pops, 171
Basil Pesto, 133
Berry Superfood Smoothie Bowls, 58
Blueberry Oatmeal with Walnuts, Banana, and Coconut, 59
Broccoli with Butternut Squash Cheese Sauce, 117
Butternut Squash Cheese Sauce, 129
Caesar Salad with Italian-Herbed Roasted Chickpeas, 75
Caribbean Jerk Tempeh Bowls, 154
Cashew Caesar Dressing, 128
Cashew Cream, 139
Cashew Hollandaise, 135
Cashew Mozzarella and Marinara Dip, 112
Chimichurri Sauce, 140
Chopped Fall Salad with Herbs, 73
Classic Chick-Free Salad, 77
Coconut Rice Pudding, 172
Cream of Broccoli Soup, 82
Easy Chana Masala, 156
Easy Guacamole, 111
Easy Overnight Oats, 60
Easy Three-Bean Chili, 86
Fried Tofu Eggs, 55
Frisée and Apple Salad with Walnuts and Pomegranate, 69
Gallo Pinto (Central American Rice and Beans), 146
Grilled Tofu and Veggie Kabobs with Chimichurri Sauce, 116
Guava Panna Cotta, 177
Hearty Vegetable Stew, 89
Italian-Herbed Roasted Chickpeas, 114
Loaded English Jacket Potatoes, 161
Mango Relish, 138
Mango Shiitake Ceviche, 76
Maple-Cinnamon Vinaigrette, 126
Mom's Homestyle Lentil Soup, 81
Mushroom-Lentil Shepherd's Pie, 160
Napa Cabbage Salad, 72
Oven Home Fries, 118
Pan-Sautéed Sweet Plantains, 119
Peanut Butter, Chocolate, and Banana Milk Shake, 175
Peanut Sauce, 131
Portobello-Pineapple Poke Bowls, 147
Portobello Steak and Tofu Eggs with Oven Home Fries, 64
Quick Cuban Black Bean Soup, 88
Quinoa-Amaranth Porridge with Dried Cranberries and Pumpkin Seeds, 57
Red Wine Vinaigrette, 126
Refried Pintos, 123
Restaurant-Style Chunky Red Salsa, 136
Roasted Beet Salad with Baby Arugula and Macadamia Ricotta, 70
Roasted Butternut Squash Soup, 87
Rustic Roasted Root Vegetables, 121
Salsa Fresca, 130

Gluten-free (*continued*)

Scrambled Tofu Eggs, 54
Seared Portobello Fajitas, 153

Southwestern Black Bean and Quinoa Bowls, 144
Spanish Rice, 122
Spiced Baked Apples with Walnuts and Oats, 174
Spiced Sweet Potato Cheesecake, 168–169
Spicy Bean Tamales, 162–163
Sweet Potato and Shiitake Mushroom Risotto, 148
Sweet Quinoa Parfait with Berries and Coconut Flakes, 176
Tex-Mex Migas, 61
Tex-Mex Tofu Scramble, 55–56
Tofu Chops with Caramelized Apple and Onion, 151
Tofu Summer Rolls, 113
Tropical Quinoa Salad, 71
20-Minute Marinara, 132
Watermelon, Cucumber, and Mint Salad, 68
Wild Mushroom and Vegetable Fried Rice, 155
Wild Rice and Lentil Stuffed Acorn Squash, 150

Nut-free

Agave-Chipotle Vinaigrette, 127
All-American Black Bean Burgers, 92–93
Apple-Sage Andouille Sausage, 109
Aquafaba Mayo, 141
Aquafaba Mint-Chocolate Mousse, 173
Avocado Toast-adas, 63
Baked Barbecue Cauliflower Wings, 115
Balsamic Reduction, 137
Blueberry Cake Donuts with Meyer Lemon Glaze, 178–179
Caribbean Island Burgers with Mango Relish, 98
Chimichurri Sauce, 140
Classic Chick-Free Salad, 77
Crispy Cauliflower Po' Boys, 100–101
Easy Chana Masala, 156
Easy Guacamole, 111
Easy Three-Bean Chili, 86
Fried Tofu Eggs, 55
Gallo Pinto (Central American Rice and Beans), 146
Grilled Tofu and Veggie Kabobs with Chimichurri Sauce, 116
Hearty Vegetable Stew, 89
Herbed Oyster Mushroom White Cream Flatbread, 158
Italian-Herbed Roasted Chickpeas, 114
Italian Sausage, 108
Italian Seitan Sausage Hoagies, 96
Jackfruit Barbecue Sandwiches, 99
Lentil Sloppy Joes, 94
Mango Relish, 138
Mango Shiitake Ceviche, 76
Maple-Cinnamon Vinaigrette, 126
Mom's Homestyle Lentil Soup, 81
Mushroom-Lentil Shepherd's Pie, 160
Oven Home Fries, 118
Pan-Sautéed Sweet Plantains, 119
Portobello-Pineapple Poke Bowls, 147
Portobello Steak and Chimichurri Sandwiches, 95
Portobello Steak and Tofu Eggs with Oven Home Fries, 64
Quinoa-Amaranth Porridge with Dried Cranberries and Pumpkin Seeds, 57
Red Wine Vinaigrette, 126
Refried Pintos, 123
Restaurant-Style Chunky Red Salsa, 136
Rustic Roasted Root Vegetables, 121
Scrambled Tofu Eggs, 54
Seared Oyster Mushroom Tortas, 102
Seitan Sausage Jambalaya, 159
Spanish Chorizo, 106–107
Spanish Chorizo and Vegetable Paella, 164–165
Spanish Rice, 122
Spicy Bean Tamales, 162–163
Tempeh Bacon, 120
Tempeh BLTs, 103
Texas-Style Barbecue Sauce, 134
Tex-Mex Migas, 61

Tex-Mex Tofu Scramble, 55–56
Tex-Mex Tortilla Soup, 85
Thick and Hearty Minestrone, 84
Tofu Chops with Caramelized Apple and Onion, 151
Tofu Egg Sandwiches, 65
20-Minute Marinara, 132
Watermelon-Mint Gazpacho, 83
Wild Mushroom and Vegetable Fried Rice, 155

Oil-free

Avocado Toast-adas, 63
Balsamic Reduction, 137
Banana Fudge Pops, 171
Berry Superfood Smoothie Bowls, 58
Blueberry Oatmeal with Walnuts, Banana, and Coconut, 59
Broccoli with Butternut Squash Cheese Sauce, 117
Butternut Squash Cheese Sauce, 129
Cashew Caesar Dressing, 128
Cashew Cream, 139
Coconut Rice Pudding, 172
Easy Guacamole, 111
Easy Overnight Oats, 60
Guava Panna Cotta, 177
Mango Relish, 138
Peanut Butter, Chocolate, and Banana Milk Shake, 175
Quinoa-Amaranth Porridge with Dried Cranberries and Pumpkin Seeds, 57
Salsa Fresca, 130
Sweet Quinoa Parfait with Berries and Coconut Flakes, 176
Watermelon, Cucumber, and Mint Salad, 68

Soy-free

Agave-Chipotle Vinaigrette, 127
Aquafaba Mayo, 141
Aquafaba Mint-Chocolate Mousse, 173
Avocado Toast-adas, 63
Balsamic Reduction, 137
Banana Fudge Pops, 171
Basil Pesto, 133
Berry Superfood Smoothie Bowls, 58
Blueberry Oatmeal with Walnuts, Banana, and Coconut, 59
Broccoli with Butternut Squash Cheese Sauce, 117
Butternut Squash Cheese Sauce, 129
Butternut Squash Mac and Cheese, 152
Cashew Caesar Dressing, 128
Cashew Cream, 139
Chimichurri Sauce, 140
Chopped Fall Salad with Herbs, 73
Classic Chick-Free Salad, 77
Coconut Rice Pudding, 172
Crostini with Macadamia Ricotta, Strawberries, and Basil, 110
Easy Chana Masala, 156
Easy Guacamole, 111
Easy Overnight Oats, 60
Frisée and Apple Salad with Walnuts and Pomegranate, 69
Gallo Pinto (Central American Rice and Beans), 146
Guava Panna Cotta, 177
Hearty Vegetable Stew, 89
Italian-Herbed Roasted Chickpeas, 114
Italian Sausage, 108
Mango Relish, 138
Mango Shiitake Ceviche, 76
Maple-Cinnamon Vinaigrette, 126
Mom's Homestyle Lentil Soup, 81
Mushroom-Lentil Shepherd's Pie, 160
Oven Home Fries, 118

Soy-free (*continued*)
Pan-Sautéed Sweet Plantains, 119
Peanut Butter, Chocolate, and Banana Milk Shake, 175
Quick Cuban Black Bean Soup, 88
Quinoa-Amaranth Porridge with Dried Cranberries and Pumpkin Seeds, 57
Red Wine Vinaigrette, 126
Refried Pintos, 123
Restaurant-Style Chunky Red Salsa, 136
Roasted Beet Salad with Baby Arugula and Macadamia Ricotta, 70
Roasted Butternut Squash Soup, 87
Rustic Roasted Root Vegetables, 121
Salsa Fresca, 130
Seared Oyster Mushroom Tortas, 102
Seitan Sausage Jambalaya, 159
Southwestern Black Bean and Quinoa Bowls, 144
Spanish Chorizo, 106–107
Spanish Rice, 122
Spicy Bean Tamales, 162–163
Sweet Quinoa Parfait with Berries and Coconut Flakes, 176
Thick and Hearty Minestrone, 84
Tropical Quinoa Salad, 71
20-Minute Marinara, 132
Watermelon, Cucumber, and Mint Salad, 68
Watermelon-Mint Gazpacho, 83
Wild Rice and Lentil Stuffed Acorn Squash, 150

Acknowledgments

In mid-2020, I lost my grandmother Soledad Benavidez. She and I shared a special bond that I will cherish forever. While she's no longer with us physically, she's always in my heart. *Te extaño, Grandma—pero en corazon estaremos juntos siempre.*

To my mom, Emma: No words can express how much I appreciate your love, generosity, and kindness. How in the world did I get so lucky to be born to someone as perfect as you? You're my hero—a true leader. A symbol of strength and compassion. I love you, Mom.

To my dad, Mike: Thank you for always being there and supporting me through thick and thin, Dad. Though you're a man of few words, your love is always on display. For as long as I can remember, you've done anything you could to help others in need—even putting others' needs ahead of your own. You inspire me to be a better human. I love you, Dad.

To my husband, Ivan: You are my rock. My best friend. My everything. I can't imagine having gone through this turbulent year without you by my side. Thank you for being my biggest fan and toughest critic. For knowing exactly when I need a push, and when I need a hug. I love you so much, *Amor*.

To my brother and sister-in-law, Michael and Erica: Thank you both for inspiring my creativity and always cheering me on. But more than anything, for providing a safe space whenever I need to get away from all the noise. Y'all are the absolute best! Sammy, I hope you know how cool your parents are.

Xiomara: Could I have asked for a better sister-friend or kitchen companion? In the words of Chi-Chi Rodriguez in *To Wong Foo*, "No, I don't think so!" Thank you for being able to read my mind in the kitch and knowing exactly when and where to jump in. But more important, thank you for being such a wonderful friend to Ivan and me. I'm forever indebted to Twist for bringing us together. *Te quiero mucho, hermanita.*

To my friend and publicist, Jasmin Espada: Thank you for always inspiring me to reach higher and higher. The cosmos brought us together, and I am so very grateful.

To my socially distant pals Ethan, Irene, Jamey, Joy, and Mark: Thank you for the jokes and rants that help keep me sane. I love you all.

About the Author

Eddie Garza is a chef, author, and program manager of food and nutrition for the Humane Society of the United States. Eddie and his work have been featured by a wide variety of media outlets in the United States and abroad, including NBC, CNN, ¡HOLA! TV, the *Washington Post*, *People*, *Travel + Leisure*, Telemundo, Univision, MiTú, Sin Embargo (Mexico), TV Azteca (Mexico), Canal Nuestra Tele (Colombia), TV Venezuela, GoTV (Honduras), *El Tiempo* and *El Colombiano* (Colombia), *Daily Mail* (United Kingdom), and many more.

Eddie has cooked for a host of plant-powered stars in the television, film, and music industries, including television host and model Daisy Fuentes; singer-songwriters Richard Marx and Rob Thomas; Latin American television personalities Marco Antonio Regil, Ximena Córdoba, and Catalina Robayo; and actors Kate Mara, Jamie Bell, Cybill Shepherd, Maria Conchita Alonso, Daniella Monet, and Harley Quinn Smith, among others.

Eddie is a sought-after speaker, culinary coach, and thought leader on issues related to plant-based health and wellness. He has lectured extensively and presented at top universities, culinary schools, and major conferences in the United States and Latin America, including South by Southwest (Austin), Expo en Verde Ser (Mexico City), and the Nexus Summit (Washington, DC).

About the Nutritionist

Lauren Pitts, MA, RD, is a registered dietitian with a masters in dietetics from the University of Oklahoma. As a leader in the plant-based nutrition field with more than eight years' experience, Lauren currently works as the National Food & Nutrition Programs Manager for the Humane Society of the United States, partnering with food service management companies, schools, universities, and hospitals to incorporate healthier, sustainable, and delicious plant-based options on their menus. She also works with healthcare professionals across the country to utilize a whole food, plant-based diet as a tool in the prevention and treatment of chronic disease. Additionally, she provides individual nutrition counseling with a passion for helping others improve their lifestyle. Lauren lives in Los Angeles and enjoys hiking, traveling, cooking, and spending time with family, friends, and her adorable dog, Rascal.

CPSIA information can be obtained
at www.ICGtesting.com
Printed in the USA
JSHW011832010221
11353JS00001B/1

9 781647 397548